HOW TO BECOME THE SUPER EMPLOYEE

Step by Step Guide to Excellence

NEERAJ BALI

INDIA • SINGAPORE • MALAYSIA

Notion Press

Old No. 38, New No. 6
McNichols Road, Chetpet
Chennai - 600 031

First Published by Notion Press 2018
Copyright © Neeraj Bali 2018
All Rights Reserved.

ISBN 978-1-64249-762-5

This book has been published with all reasonable efforts taken to make the material error-free after the consent of the author. No part of this book shall be used, reproduced in any manner whatsoever without written permission from the author, except in the case of brief quotations embodied in critical articles and reviews.

The Author of this book is solely responsible and liable for its content including but not limited to the views, representations, descriptions, statements, information, opinions and references ["Content"]. The Content of this book shall not constitute or be construed or deemed to reflect the opinion or expression of the Publisher or Editor. Neither the Publisher nor Editor endorse or approve the Content of this book or guarantee the reliability, accuracy or completeness of the Content published herein and do not make any representations or warranties of any kind, express or implied, including but not limited to the implied warranties of merchantability, fitness for a particular purpose. The Publisher and Editor shall not be liable whatsoever for any errors, omissions, whether such errors or omissions result from negligence, accident, or any other cause or claims for loss or damages of any kind, including without limitation, indirect or consequential loss or damage arising out of use, inability to use, or about the reliability, accuracy or sufficiency of the information contained in this book.

Dedicated to
My Two Gurus Govind & Gobind

Govind, also known as Lord Krishna, taught us the greatest teachings of life in the battle of Kurukshetra, which are compiled in the holy book of *Bhagavad Gita*.

Gobind, also known as Guru Gobind Singh ji, demonstrated great leadership and sacrificed his father, four sons, mother & self for the defense of humanity against the Mughal assault of Aurangzeb.

Our past, present and future generations will always be indebted to them.

> The ideas I stand for are not mine. I borrowed them from Socrates. I swiped them from Chesterfield. I stole them from Jesus. And I put them in a book. If you don't like their rules, whose would you use?
>
> – Dale Carnegie

CONTENTS

Preface .... *ix*
Acknowledgements..................................... *xi*

Section A - Mind Empowerment

1. What Is Your Why? 3
2. Ask for What You Want..............................11
3. Believe It Is Possible 13
4. What Is Your Plan?..................................17
5. Be a Goal Setter....................................21
6. Two Great Attitudes toward Workplace..................27
7. Be Thankful for Problems............................29
8. Love to Be a Problem Solver 33
9. Magic of Visualisation...............................41
10. Face Failure Fearlessly 45
11. Most Powerful Law of Success........................49
12. Mentoring..59
13. Look for Stars, Not for Darkness 63
14. Invest in Yourself Continually 67
15. Association Makes All the Difference 71
16. Take Pride in Your Work 75
17. Be Honest with Your Work 79
18. Your Growth Stopper Has Died 83

Section B - Skill Empowerment

19. Do You Brush Your Teeth Every Day?...................87
20. Not Changing Is Not an Option 91
21. Ask Yourself Empowering Questions 97
22. Learn People Skills 103
23. Be a Great Networker 107
24. Learn One New Skill Each Year 111
25. Leverage Technology to Increase Productivity 115
26. Learn to Be Good at Selling.........................119
27. Never Say No......................................123
28. Become More Valuable 125

Section C - Action Empowerment

29. Be the First One to Do It............................133
30. Be Focused on Your KRAs..........................135
31. All Do It Some. Some Do It All.......................137
32. Dare to Accept Responsibility.......................139
33. Let's Embrace Risks................................141
34. Ask for Help 147
35. Be Known for Your Work Culture 151
36. Can You See Your Mistakes? 153
37. How Badly Do You Know Your Product?...............155
38. Be a Continuous "Work in Progress" 157
39. Are You Preparing for the Next Level? 159

Section D - Discipline Empowerment

40. Never Start Your Day Unless.....…..................165
41. Focus on Priorities 169
42. Learn to Say No Every Day. Period...................173

43. Most Powerful Habit for Productivity..................177

44. Do Monthly Review with Your Boss 181

45. Never End Your Day Unless... 185

46. Work Hard, Start Early, Stay Later....................187

47. Magic Pill before You Sleep 191

48. Self-Discipline and Accountability 195

49. Never Give Up 199

PREFACE

I want you to be among the 1%

Right after my MBA, because of the gap between job expectations and job reality, I sunk into depression. I joined my first job while I was in that phase, acting as if everything was alright. I suffered a lot of pain due to mistakes made consciously and unconsciously in the first 4–5 years, in the absence of professional coaching and mentoring. I don't want this pain to happen to anyone else.

Like how mothers have to be extremely careful about their baby in the first 4–5 months of pregnancy, you also have to be extra careful when you have just begun a job. These years are the deciding years for winners, to set the height you will reach in your career.

Only 1% of people have a career that grows under professional coaching, mentoring and handholding. They are the people who are not afraid of making mistakes, face maximum fears, stretch the most, sacrifice the most and finally win the most. That's how they become the super-employees of their companies, and I want you to be among that 1%.

Would you like to be among that 1%? Would you like to know and do what that 1% does? READ THIS BOOK

This book is a compilation of experiences and advices of CEOs, HR managers, Top performers, Entrepreneurs and Spiritualists. It includes the best practices of top performers of different industries who have succeeded faster than others, who have got the maximum and fastest promotions in their careers and have been paid much more than others.

Finally, if I have to summarise it, this book is written with the intention of being your coach, mentor and guide on your career journey to becoming one of the 1%.

So the Million Dollar question is: DO YOU WANT TO BE AMONG THE 1% CALLED SUPER-EMPLOYEES?

If yes, then start your journey, and live this book.

ACKNOWLEDGEMENTS

First I must thank GOD for giving me an idea, guidance & courage for how I wish to be of service to you.

To all those philosophers, theologians and prophets who contributed to the *Bhagavad Gita, Quran* and the *Bible*.

To Napoleon Hill, for his observation on success and starting this self-help industry and laws of success.

To the author of the book *The Secret*, Rhonda Byrne, based on the law of attraction, who took the works of Abraham Hicks to the next level and made *The Secret* a household item, a book which is part of every dreamer's survival kit.

To Dale Carnegie from whom I learnt the basic of human engineering, the power of appreciation, the power of smiling and the courage to admit mistakes. No doubt I call him the "Father of Human engineering."

Thank you to legends like Jim Rohn, Brian Tracy, Jack Canfield, Anthony Robbins and Les Brown, from whom I have learnt a lot through their articles, books and speaking assignments.

Deepest gratitude to all those great human beings of centuries ago and till today, who discovered the truths of life and who left their written words so that we might discover them at exactly the right time.

Thank you to My Father Mr. R C Bali & My Mother Tejinder Kaur whose simplicity and sacrifices have always been an inspiration to do well in my life and make them proud through my work.

Thank you to my sister Namrata, whose writing has always been an inspiration for many of our family and friends. This book is an attempt to awaken the sleeping writer in her.

Thanks to my entrepreneur brother Deepak who was always a helping hand, listening ear and is true to his name, as he always lights up my way.

Thanks to all my seniors, mentors and trainer colleagues, with special reference to Anubhuti who so gracefully imparted their knowledge and experiences to me.

Thanks to my daughter Vrinda who always believed in me and asked, "Papa when will be your book be completed?" whenever we would go to a book shop, and when she would see some bestselling book hanging there, she always would say, "Papa, your book will also be hanging like this one day here." In between, while writing this book, I lost an important file where many of the chapters were written. It was a great blow to me, as I was in a fix as to how to retain all those chapters and content, but she consistently prayed for me all those 3 months, and finally, GOD helped me to get that lost file. Perhaps, GOD could not refuse the prayers of such little angels. Thank you, Vrinda.

Thanks to my wife, Sucheta, who sacrificed a lot to help me write and complete this book.

Thanks to my editor Ms. Sushmita, my project manager Mr. Arun & the entire Notion Press team for telling me to my face where I needed correction. To my younger brother Vineet Sharma who understood my passion for self-development, entrepreneurship and introduced and guided me to the world of Kindle, blogging and building a career in writing.

Thanks to every source from whom I learnt, and I seek forgiveness if I missed acknowledging someone who contributed in this journey.

The information provided in this book is designed to provide helpful information on the subjects discussed. I the author of this book ask for forgiveness for any mistake or error I may have overlooked while writing this book.

SECTION A - MIND EMPOWERMENT

CHAPTER 1
WHAT IS YOUR WHY?

"Most Important and most missed ingredient in the recipe of success is WHY."

— Neeraj Bali

All my life, I had been in search of a universal question. "What is the Number 1 factor responsible for mega success in any person's life?" And all answers taught to me has changed from time to time till I discovered the real one few years ago.

Instead of telling you, let me facilitate you through 2 real life stories, which will open to you the Number 1 factor responsible for mega success in any person's life.

FIRST STORY

Can you believe this? A poor man living in a remote village in India, hardly able to earn enough for three meals a day, decided to cut through a mountain and connect two villages that were on either side.

Due to the mountain, villagers had to go through a very long route along its peripheries to go from one village to another. If the mountain could be removed and a way be made through it, the distance would be reduced from 70 km to 1 km.

He proposed his idea to all the villagers, who called him a fool and ridiculed him. Who could move a mountain? Moreover, who has that much time? Who could possibly have enough strength to actually do it?

Against the wishes of his family and without getting any support from the village, community or government, he took a decision to break the mountain and carve a path between the two villages.

This decision changed his destiny.

Meet Dashrath Manjhi, a native of Gahlor village near Gaya district in Bihar (India).

Dashrath Manjhi sold his goats and bought a hammer and chisel. With just those tools, he started working on it despite mockery and all odds. Years passed, during which his village was hit by a massive drought and everyone was evacuated.

Dashrath's father taunted him and asked him what he had achieved in so many years. He tried to convince Dashrath to accompany them to a city, where he could earn bread for his two children. But, Dashrath decided to continue his herculean task. With no water or food, Dashrath was forced to drink dirty water and eat leaves.

After 22 years, Dashrath Manjhi single-mindedly, without any support and against all odds, did the unbelievable. He single-handedly carved a 360 foot long (110 m), 25 foot high (7.6 m) and 30 foot wide (9.1 m) road by cutting through a mountain for 22 years.

Dashrath moved the mountain.

He became an overnight success after 22 years of madness. The villagers, his community, the state government and the whole country appreciated him for his noble work. Finally, the government joined him in his noble work at the last stage and helped him fulfil his dream.

Articles in every newspaper and magazine were written on him and his mission. A documentary film was made on his life called *Manjhi - The Mountain Man.* I highly recommend this movie to everyone. It will change your life.

WHY OF DASHRATH MANJHI

Can you imagine why he was able to do this consistently for 22 years despite all odds? Let me narrate the reason WHY.

One day, Falguni, who was heavily pregnant, was taking lunch for her husband to the fields, for which she needed to climb the mountain in the scorching heat. Unfortunately, Falguni's foot slipped, and she fell down while hungry Dashrath was waiting for the food. Then, someone from the village alerted Dashrath that his wife had fallen down from the mountain.

Dashrath ran desperately and took his blood-splattered wife to the nearest hospital that was 70 km away. There, he was told that he had come too late and that his wife was dead on arrival. However, their baby had survived.

REVENGE BEGINS

Heartbroken, Manjhi held the mountain responsible for his wife's death, and he took the decision to remove it and carve a path between the two villages so that nobody else should have to suffer like his wife.

This kept running Dashrath for 22 years.

This became the purpose for Dashrath for 22 years.

This became the driving force for Dashrath for 22 years.

This became the Dashrath's WHY for 22 years and made him a superhuman who moved the mountain.

What is your WHY to become the SUPER EMPLOYEE of your organisation?

SECOND STORY

Let me take you to the second incident which changed the course of history in the travel industry. In his book, *Start with Why,* Simon beautifully derived this fundamental principle. I highly recommend this book, *Start with Why,* to anyone who wants to take his growth to an exponential level. This story shared below is taken from Simon's book *Start with Why.*

Simon shared an incident that occurred in the 20th century, when the possibility of a flying machine was being contemplated. A machine that could fly like birds and change the course of mankind. A machine that we call aeroplanes today.

Among many, two teams were seriously working on it – Samuel Pierpont Langley (SPL) and Wright Brothers.

SPL was given 50,000 dollars by the war department to figure out this flying machine. Money was no problem. He had a seat at Harvard and worked at Smithsonian. He was extremely well connected. He knew the big minds of the day. He hired the best minds money could find, & market conditions were also fantastic. *The New York Times* followed him around everywhere, and everyone was rooting for SPL.

On the other side, a few hundred miles away in Dayton, Ohio, Orville & Wilbur Wright had none of what SPL was having. They had no money, so they paid for their dreams with the proceeds from their bicycle shop. Not a single person from the Wright Brothers team had a college education, not even Orville or Wilbur.

SPL had every probable ingredient of success. Money, brain, connections and back up. But how come most people don't know about SPL & history remembers the Wright Brothers only? How come only the Wright Brothers succeeded despite all odds? Where was the difference?

Wright Brothers were driven by a cause, by a purpose, by a belief that if they could figure out this flying machine, it would change the course of the world and reduce the physical distances. The people who believed in the Wright Brothers dreamed and worked with them with blood, sweat and tears.

On the other hand, the driving force for SPL was different. He wanted to be rich, famous and the first one to invent it. The people who worked for SPL worked for cheques.

And eventually on Dec 17, 1983, the Wright Brothers took flight when no one was there to experience it. And further proof that SPL was motivated by wrong thing is that the day the Wright Brothers invented the flying machine, SPL stopped working on the flying machine project instead of congratulating the Wright Brothers and collaborating with them and offering his services for further development.

The difference between the Wright Brothers and SPL was in their purpose.

The difference was in their driving force.

The difference was in their WHY.

So what is your driving force to keep you working against all odds?

What is your purpose that will keep you running?

What is your WHY to become the SUPER EMPLOYEE of your organisation?

So what have we learned from the above real life stories? Were the tasks normal? Were the challenges normal? How did they do it?

Because their WHY was crystal clear.

On your journey towards excellence, you need to check out certain things about your WHY.

- **Is your WHY a challenging one and a big one?**
- **Is your WHY an emotional one?**
- **Is your WHY driven with a purpose?**

For example: If you say you want 10 lakh dollars in the next 3 years because you want to buy your dad a house, it is great. Your WHY is now a challenging one, emotionally connected with sentiments and driven with a purpose.

This is because when your WHY is big, challenging, emotional and driven with a purpose, it will provide you the strength, energy and drive to overcome tough days, to make sacrifices, to make those tough decisions, to say NO to many things and to go out of your comfort zone. Only because of this you will be able to continue your journey despite all odds.

Your WHY has to be bigger than your fear of failure, discomfort and challenges.

The most common missing ingredient in recipe of Success is WHY. Why do you want to do it? The biggest reason people fail is because they forgot to put this in. We do everything – planning, coaching, reviewing, however, we miss the most important ingredient. All the highly successful people discovered their WHY before they fulfilled their dreams.

So, what is your purpose for becoming the SUPER EMPLOYEE?

Is it the financial raise only (like everyone wants)? What will you do with that money?

Is it the honour? Whom would you dedicate that success to? Never underestimate the power of honour. A soldier puts his life on stake in a battle for a medal on his uniform, which financially does not cost more than perhaps Rs. 10,000 in the market. But, he sometimes sacrifices his life for the honour of that medal.

Does it challenge the status quo? For example: Getting the fastest promotion in the shortest period.

What is your Why for becoming the SUPER EMPLOYEE of your organisation?

So, find out your WHY, which is emotional and big enough, which can make you rise from the bed before the sun rises, which can fill your eyes with tears, which can fill your heart with passion and which can fill your muscles with power every time you fall down. That why will keep you running on your journey, and that WHY will make you the SUPER EMPLOYEE of your organisation.

> "He who has a WHY to live for can bear almost any HOW."
> – Friedrich Nietzsche

CHAPTER 2
ASK FOR WHAT YOU WANT

"Ask & you shall receive."

One of the best lessons I learned from my career as a corporate trainer is **Expectation Mapping.** At the start of every Training Session, I used to do the expectation mapping with my audience, which involved asking what they were expecting from the session & explaining what they would learn from the training. Right at the beginning stage, the expected outcome would be clear to both parties, and if any difference was there, it would be corrected at the very first step. **If we can do expectation mapping for a small training session, why can't we do expectation mapping for the most important event of our career, which is career growth?**

Let's see how it will work in your career. Say you have a goal to get promoted in a year and become a team leader. Go to your boss, tell him this is what you have set as a goal and that you have understood your current roles and responsibilities. Apart from this, mention your other expectations. Learn his expectations of the person who will hold this post. This is even more important where clear roles and responsibilities are not defined.

Share your expectations from your boss. If you require help, ask for it. If it is regular feedback on progress or mistakes, fix the date for asking it. If it is a monthly review or counselling at regular intervals, fix the date for it.

ADVANTAGES OF EXPECTATION MAPPING

Doing expectation mapping right at beginning will ensure least surprise factor, least communication gaps and least deviation in the journey. This will keep the progress on the right track, right direction and at the right speed. Don't be scared that your Boss might say NO. Ask politely why not? He may tell you all your weaknesses. You can improve on them. At least you are now clear right from the beginning.

Sometimes, fear may come in your mind. You may fear what your boss will think. He will appreciate this daring step and will keep correcting you when you are deviating from it. Your boss will also know that you are expecting a bigger role and that you are working hard for it. He will be happy about it. So, go ahead with a full plan. Do it.

Having a clear and agreed expectation mapping right at the beginning will keep your progress on the right track, right direction and at the right speed, and that is how you will become the SUPER EMPLOYEE of your organisation.

ANECDOTE

Interviewer: Where do you see yourself 2 years from now?
Candidate: On the seat you are sitting on.

ACTIONABLE

Have you shared your goal to your immediate supervisor? Have you done the expectation mapping with your boss? If not, just do it.

CHAPTER 3
BELIEVE IT IS POSSIBLE

"We are all born to succeed but programmed to fail."

Will you start a journey where deep inside you believe that that you will not reach the destination?

Will you start a business where deep inside you believe that you will not be successful in that business?

The chances are that you and I will not. So the belief in your abilities and belief in getting success is among the foundational steps for success anywhere and everywhere.

HOW ARE BELIEFS MADE?

I read somewhere on the Internet that beliefs are like the unquestioned commands given to the brain and that our brain blindly obeys that command and accordingly gives instructions to different parts of the body. A belief is nothing but a final interpretation you have drawn of some events in your life. It may be true, and it may be false, but you have accepted it as a final truth in your life.

For example: When a child is learning to ride the bicycle and falls 3–4 times while learning. He might get a little injury also. Now, if not properly coached, encouraged and guided by parents at this stage, the child might develop a belief that he cannot learn how to ride the bicycle, and consequently, he might not make future attempts, and finally, he might give up.

Beliefs can be empowering one hand and disempowering on the other. The good news is that beliefs can be changed from disempowering to empowering.

HOW NEW AND EMPOWERING BELIEFS ARE MADE

If you study the life of the great boxer Muhammad Ali, you will find a very interesting aspect of his career. Muhammad Ali stated, "I am the greatest, I said that even before I knew I was." Like him, by giving consistent positive affirmations to your subconscious mind followed by other success principles, you can create a new empowering belief. Initially, it might sound fake, but gradually, with consistent commands to the subconscious mind along with following other basic principles, it becomes reality. That's why we say, "Fake it till you make it."

I highly recommend the book *What to Say When You Talk to Your Self.* This book talks about how, unconsciously, our internal dialogues affect our performance and how we can use this science to accelerate our performance.

Having a positive & empowering belief is very important because belief impacts your behaviour and performance. Let me share the inspiring real life story of Roger Bannister to demonstrate my point.

Sir Roger Bannister was the first man in history to run a mile in under four minutes. Up until he did it in 1954, most people thought the four-minute mark was impossible to break. It was believed that the human body couldn't physically go that fast – that it would collapse under the pressure.

It was believed to be an impossible task to run a mile in less than four minutes.

That was until Bannister proved everyone wrong.

And yet, just 46 days after Bannister broke the record, Landy beat his time.

Over the next few years, more and more people broke the four-minute mark once they realised that yes, it was possible.

Once Bannister proved that it was possible to run a mile in under four minutes, suddenly everyone was able to do it, proving an important lesson: **once you start believing something is possible, it becomes possible.**

Find out your disempowering beliefs. Replace them with empowering beliefs like Muhammad Ali did, and that is how you will become the SUPER EMPLOYEE of your organisation.

"Man often becomes what he believes himself to be. If I keep on saying to myself that I cannot do a certain thing, it is possible that I may end by really becoming incapable of doing it. On the contrary, if I shall have the belief that I can do it, I shall surely acquire the capacity to do it, even if I may not have it at the beginning."

– Mahatma Gandhi

CHAPTER 4
WHAT IS YOUR PLAN?

"Most people don't plan to fail; they fail to plan."

- John L. Beckley

The second most missed principle in the recipe of success is planning. We are all sincere. We all work hard & want to progress in life. But, we underestimate the importance of planning. We work hard without hard planning behind that work. That's perhaps why Henry Ford said, "Thinking is the hardest work there is, which is probably the reason why so few engage in it."

Albert Einstein was once asked, "If there was a major emergency or potential disaster that was going to destroy the earth in 60 minutes, and you were asked to find a solution, what would you do?"

Einstein replied, "I would spend the first 59 minutes gathering information, and the last minute solving the problem in the best possible way."

Likewise, Abraham Lincoln perhaps wanted to convey the same message when he said, "If I had 24 hours to chop a tree, I would spend 18 hours in sharpening the axe."

If you think that you don't care about this planning thing then wait for some time, your boss will make a plan for you. That's how he has become a boss. So, it's better to understand the importance of planning and execute it toward achieving every goal which is important for your career growth.

Planning will increase your preparation level. In turn, preparation will increase your confidence level. Your confidence will reduce your stress level and will keep you fit and ready for future challenges.

Brian Tracy very beautifully expressed, "Every minute you spend in planning saves 10 minutes in execution; this gives you a 1,000 percent Return on Energy!" That's one of the most profitable investments you can do for your career growth.

If a million dollar company plans monthly, quarterly, half yearly, annually… don't you think you and me also need to plan our careers?

Your promotion will not happen by default. You have to earn it. And to earn it, among the first few steps is planning for it.

Planning includes the clear understanding of knowing what to achieve in how much time.

Planning includes the clear understanding of knowing what skills to achieve.

Planning includes the clear understanding of knowing how to plan your day, week and month in advance.

Planning includes the clear understanding that you need to review every day.

Planning includes the clear understanding of setting milestones and having plans to achieve them.

If you take care of planning, planning will take care of your future. So never start your day, unless you have planned it on paper. Do it religiously every day, every week, every month, and that is how you will become the SUPER EMPLOYEE of your organisation.

> "The best way to predict your future is to plan it."

CHAPTER 5
BE A GOAL SETTER

*"It must be borne in mind that the tragedy
of life doesn't lie in not reaching your goal.
The tragedy lies in having no goals to reach."*

– Benjamin E. Mays

In the book *What They Don't Teach You at Harvard Business School*, Mark McCormack discusses a study conducted on students in the 1979 Harvard MBA programme. In that year, the students were asked, "Have you set clear, written goals for your future and made plans to accomplish them?" Only three percent of the graduates had written goals and plans; 13 percent had goals, but they were not in writing; and a whopping 84 percent had no specific goals at all.

Ten years later, the members of the class were interviewed again, and the findings, while somewhat predictable, were nonetheless astonishing. The 13 percent of the class who had goals were earning, on average, twice as much as the 84 percent who had no goals at all. And what about the three percent who had clear, written goals? They were earning, on average, ten times as much as the other 97 percent put together.

In spite of such proof of success, most people don't have clear, measurable, time-bounded goals that they work toward.

Recently, I read an article where this beautiful piece of wisdom was written by Com Mirza, CEO of Fitness Expo Dubai:

> "Write goals five times a day, every day. I believe in conditioning my mindset and belief system by writing my goals out five times a day. I set reminders on my iPhone and never skip a single day. This helps me condition the mind, and reformat my thoughts to continually focus on my dreams and goals. By writing every day, I force my mind to cancel the noise, distractions and random thoughts in order to focus intensely on my dreams and goals. Try it for a week and see for yourself how powerful this technique is."

I don't know how goal setting and writing your goals work, but I know one thing – IT CERTAINLY WORKS.

Perhaps it gives us direction, keeps us focused, brings out the best from us, creates a roadmap for success, gives us the motivation, pushes us and helps us to prioritise.

Or perhaps it works like the way it was mentioned in a blog on timesthought.com. The article is titled *SMART Goals: How to Set and Achieve Them.* Here is what it said:

> *Your goal statement should be a clear and specific statement of what you want.*
>
> *The main reason is that your brain behaves like a goal-seeking mechanism, similar to a precision guided missile. As these missiles fly, they continually make small adjustments and corrections to their trajectories to realign themselves to their target.*

Your brain also works in a similar way. Dr. Maxwell Maltz, author of the classic Psycho-Cybernetics, said that human beings have a built-in goal-seeking "success mechanism" that is part of the subconscious mind.

This success mechanism is constantly searching for ways to help us reach our targets and find answers to our problems. According to Maltz, we work and feel better when our success mechanism is fully engaged going after clear targets.

All we have to do to use this mechanism is to give it a specific target. Without one, our success mechanism lies dormant, or worse, pursues targets we didn't consciously choose.

When your target is vague or ambiguous, your success mechanism can become confused and either shut down or go after the wrong target.

Over a period of time, I have learned that the goal setting exercise must have certain characteristics. Below are the 4 important characteristics:

- **Set a challenging goal:** Your goal should be a challenging and big one. It should scare you a little when you think about it, and when you visualise achieving it, it should excite you a lot.
- **Link your goal with your WHY:** Your goal should be emotional and connected with a purpose. Your goals should be connected with your WHY. As we discussed in the previous chapter, your WHY will give you the extra power to achieve your goal.

- **Keep your goal before your eyes:** One of the very simple but very powerful lessons I learned from goal setting is keeping your goals before your eyes, keeping it in a place where you can see it many times a day. Perhaps one such place can be your work station. Paste your goal on your work station. This is perhaps one place where you spend maximum time. Otherwise, out of sight out of mind. Let's take a small example to understand this. Suppose your goal is to drink 4 litres of water in the next 8 hours. If you keep this goal just in mind, chances are very high that you will end up drinking 1 litre only. However, if you keep a water bottle on your work station, it will constantly remind you of your goal, and chances are very high that you will end up drinking either 3 litres or complete 4 litres. So, that's why experts advise to keep it before your eyes.

- **Set SMART Goals:** SMART is an acronym in which S means Smart, M means Measureable, A means Attainable, R means Realistic and T means Time-Bound. When you set a goal to get promoted to the next managerial designation with a minimum 12% increment in the next 12 months, this is a goal which is specific, measurable, attainable, realistic and time-bound. You have given a clear set of instructions to your subconscious mind. Now, the chances of attaining this goal will be very high.

What will happen if you don't set your goals? Your boss will set it for you. It has to be there in your success recipe. The only choice is who will put this ingredient – you or your boss.

My ex-boss Sandeep Punj always used to remind his team, "Give clear goals to your mind, else it will make your life hell."

How you live your day shows how you live your life. So the key to achieve lifetime goals is to achieve daily goals.

So set goals every day.

- **If you achieve everyday goals, you will achieve weekly goals.**
- **If you achieve weekly goals, you will achieve monthly goals.**
- **If you achieve monthly goals, you will achieve quarterly goals.**
- **If you achieve quarterly goals, you will achieve annual goals.**

And if you achieve your annual goals, that is how you will become the SUPER EMPLOYEE of your organisation.

> "By recording your dreams and goals on paper, you set in motion the process of becoming the person you most want to be. Put your future in good hands—your own."
>
> - Mark Victor Hansen

Actionable: Write your Most Important goal 5 times every day.

CHAPTER 6

TWO GREAT ATTITUDES TOWARD WORKPLACE

"The only disability in life is a bad attitude."

- Scott Hamilton

My ex-boss Abul Sir often shares this priceless piece of wisdom, which he learned from his father, in many of his training sessions. It is about 2 great attitudes toward the workplace. This chapter is dedicated to the same old person who was not an academically qualified person but someone who knew something rarely taught in any business school. It helped a lot in my career.

He used to say to Abul Sir, "Abul, wherever you work, in whatever capacity you work, always remember these 2 attitudes."

1st Attitude: If you are an employee, work as if you are the owner.

Think of everything from an ownership angle. **Think ownership. Breathe ownership. Act ownership.**

2nd Attitude: If you are an owner or boss, work as if you are the employee and like you are accountable to someone. Set good leadership examples before your shareholders and staff.

I can bet on my life, whatever maybe the country, whatever may be the industry, whatever may be the department, these 2 attitudes will always shine, and if you stick to them and follow them religiously, they will keep your productivity at an all-time high level. However, we will talk about the 1st attitude in this chapter.

In our corporate career, many times we come across situations when we have to take a tough decision, when we are scared, when we feel confused, when we don't have enough time or resources to postpone that moment and ask for help. You have to take a decision, then and there. In that tense situation, just close your eyes, take a deep breath and ask yourself, "What would the owner of the company have decided in this situation?" And just do that. Chances are high that eight out of ten times, you will be right. And in other 2 cases, you will always be relaxed that at least your intent was right.

Many times, I came across many employees who refused to think out of their department. They will prefer sitting idle but not ready to stretch themselves out of their comfort zone and learn a little, help a little. My serious request: **Think beyond "that's not my job."** If you will never outgo, you will never outgrow.

One of the great benefits of Ownership Mentality Attitude is that you will get wisdom, courage and clarity to take right decisions and right steps in the right direction, irrespective of whether someone likes it or not. And that is how you will become the SUPER EMPLOYEE of your organisation.

> I wake up every morning and think to myself, 'How far can I push the company forward in the next 24 hours?'
> - Leah Busque, CEO & Founder, Task Rabbit

CHAPTER 7
BE THANKFUL FOR PROBLEMS

"Problem is not the problem. Your attitude towards the problem is the real problem."

In my career and personal life, I have gone through and grown through understanding 4 levels of reactions towards problems. As an employee, the faster you leave the first two levels and move to the third level, the faster will your growth happen. And nothing like if you can enter into 4th level of reaction towards problems. In fact, the fourth level is not reaction, it's pro-activeness. Let's see and understand these 4 levels.

Level 1: Resisting problems
Level 2: Complaining about problems
Level 3: Being grateful for problems
Level 4: Looking for problems

Level 1: Resisting problems: This was the stage when I used to wonder why all problems happened to me only. *Why me?* Then, over a period of time, I understood that it happens with everyone. Nobody is immune to them. In fact, I should be happy that problems are happening to me because the only people who never face problems are the ones under graves.

Level 2: Complaining about problems: This was the stage when I started accepting problems but could never see anything good in it. Problem solving was always clubbed with complaining. After being coached by my seniors and mentors, my attitude towards accepting problems changed. I realised that problems are actually the reasons for our progress. No problems means no progress.

Walking was a problem, so someone invented the wheel.

Travelling by road took so much time, so the Wright Brothers invented the flying machine.

Petrol scarcity is a challenge, so we now have electric cars in every country.

All progress by mankind has happened because someone identified the problem, and instead of complaining against it, he started working for its solution.

So after I understood this, more than half of my complaining nature was gone and my transition to level 3 happened.

Level 3: Being grateful for problems: This is the stage when I started looking for positives in negatives, good in bad and opportunities in problems. Whenever I face any problem, I ask myself, "What's good in it?" "How can I convert this situation into an opportunity?" Initially, my brain resists, but after sometime, he starts giving me beautiful answers that give me power and logic to solve that problem.

Now, I believe that we should be thankful if we are given a harder job than we like because a razor cannot be sharpened on a piece of velvet. See the problems like a washing machine. They twist, they spin & knock us around. But in the end, we come out cleaner, brighter & better than before. A smooth sea never made a skilful sailor. So let's be thankful for the problems and try to see the positive in every problem. Being human, I still miss this level sometimes and go back to level 2, but most of the time, I try to remain in level 3.

Level 4: Looking for Problems: Since childhood, I would see an inspirational poster from Archies that I never understood till the age of 35. It used to say, "If you are looking for a big opportunity, find out a big problem." Now I have understood it, and this is actually level 4. This is the level which less than 1% of people enter into.

Here people are proactively going toward finding out problems, finding their solutions and converting them into business opportunities and making great business organisations out of them. Generally, entrepreneurs fall into this category. This is the level which I have not entered so far, but actually started taking baby steps toward.

Now our growth in life, career or anywhere will depend on the level we are into and how fast we can upgrade to the next level. But my sincere advice, enter into level 3 as fast as possible.

So the next time you face a problem, immediately say Thank GOD for giving this opportunity, for this gift to strengthen my ability, to polish my skills, for showing me the next step on the promotional ladder, and that is how you will become the SUPER EMPLOYEE of your organisation.

I would like to end this chapter with an expansion of the word PROBLEM. It is a real definition of problems in the minds of winners and champions, and it is how you and me should see problems as:

> Problems are PURPOSEFUL ROADBLOCKS OFFERING BENEFICIAL LESSONS TO ENHANCE MENTAL STRENGTH.

CHAPTER 8

LOVE TO BE A PROBLEM SOLVER

"All life is problem solving."

— Karl R. Popper

Before I share my experiences and learning on how to be a problem solver, first I think it is more important to understand why it is more important to be a problem solver.

Why should you love to be a problem solver?

Because the world is full of problem tellers. There is no talent required in becoming a problem teller. All the recognition, awards and growth goes to the problem solver.

Your problem-solving attitude and skills will increase your reputation, your credibility, your confidence, your brand value and puts you on a fast track path for your future growth and future leadership roles. So love to be a problem solver, see the problems as opportunities to showcase yourself. Only then you will tackle them positively and will be able to find out solutions.

Don't pray for a problem-free life. It never existed for anyone, and it will never exist. Pray for wisdom, strength and skills to become a problem solver.

LET ME SHARE A VERY BEAUTIFUL STORY

Ajay lived in a small city in Rajasthan (India). He was a graduate and worked with a private company, but he was not happy. Suffering from a pessimistic attitude, Ajay was always worried about the problems in his life. Someone told him about a saint in the township near the ashram, who would solve all problems. Ajay decided to meet this saint.

So, on Sunday, he went to visit the saint. After a long wait, he finally got a chance to meet the saint. Ajay visited the saint and said, "Master, I am surrounded by problems all the time. Sometimes there are problems at the office, sometimes at home and sometimes ill health keeps me worried. Master, kindly state such a measure with which all my problems will be gone and I can live in peace."

The saint smiled and said, "Dear, it is too late today. The night has begun to fall. I will answer your question tomorrow morning, but will you please do me a little favour?"

"Yes, of course!" said Ajay. The saint said, "Look, we have one hundred camels in the Ashram enclosure. Their caretaker fell sick today. I want you to take care of these camels tonight. When all the 100 camels go to sleep, you also go to sleep. Saying this, the Saint moved into his room.

The next day, the Saint met Ajay and asked, "Say dear, did you sleep well at night?"

Ajay replied in a very sad tone, "Master, I could not sleep even for a moment. I tried a lot, but all the camels were never seated. One or the other camel kept standing all night." Hearing this, the saint smiled and said, "I knew it would be the case. Last night you saw no matter how much you try, you cannot make all the camels sit together. If you make one sit, the other will stand. Problems are also like these camels. You will solve one problem, another will stem out from somewhere. Therefore, it is better to learn to enjoy life in spite of these problems. Yesterday, you must have noticed that many camels sat down themselves after standing for a while, some sat after your efforts, and some did not sit even after your regular efforts. Similarly, some problems are solved by efforts, some solve themselves with time. You should leave such problems to time. Learn to be happy. Sleep without worries. When the appropriate time comes, problems will themselves be solved."

Now let's see step by step how we can be good problem solvers:

STEP 1: START WITH BELIEF

All discoveries done till now, all mysteries solved till now, all wars won till now, had only been possible because it was believed at the very beginning that they might be difficult but possible to achieve. Without the belief, achieving success is not possible. In fact, achieving success is a far-off thing; you will not start taking action if deep inside you believe it is not possible.

Have you ever wondered, seeing a huge giant elephant tied to a small weak pole in a circus complex? An adult elephant can easily uproot the pole and run away, but he does not; in fact he never tries. This is because he does not believe he has the strength to uproot the pole. The reason behind this is that he was tied to the pole since he was an infant. At that time, his strength was very less. So even if he tried at that time, he could not uproot it and failed many times. Since then, he believed that he can never uproot it. But that poor soul does not know that on growing old, his strength probably has increased by 100 times. But because of his old belief, he never tries and remains stuck to that old, small, weak pole, despite having all the power.

Likewise, you might have all the power, wisdom, resources to solve the problem, but if you don't believe you can do it, you will never try and never be able to be a problem solver.

STEP 2: HAVE YOU UNDERSTOOD THE PROBLEM CLEARLY?

Charles Kettering, the famed inventor and head of research for GM, put it very beautifully. He said, "A Problem well-stated is half-solved."

The second most important factor after belief is understanding the problem in the right capacity and right dimensions. Only then you will be able to solve it in the least time, with least effort and least resources. Sometimes we unnecessarily see the problem in a big size, in a complex way which drains our energy, scares unnecessarily and weakens our ability to solve it. Let me share an anecdote to illustrate this point.

One fine day, a bus driver went to the bus garage, started his bus, and drove off along the route.

No problems for the first few stops – a few people got on, a few got off, and things went generally well.

At the next stop, however, a big hulk of a guy got on.

Six feet eight, built like a wrestler, arms hanging down to the ground.

He glared at the driver and said, "Big John doesn't need to pay!" and sat down at the back.

Did I mention that the driver was five feet three, thin, and basically meek? Well, he was.

Naturally, he didn't argue with Big John, but he wasn't happy about it.

The next day the same thing happened-Big John got on again, made a show of refusing to pay, and sat down.

And the next day, and the one after that and so forth.

This grated on the bus driver, who started losing sleep over the way Big John was taking advantage of him.

Finally, he could stand it no longer.

He signed up for body building courses, karate, judo, and all that good stuff.

By the end of the summer, he had become quite strong; what's more, he felt really good about himself.

So on the next Monday, when Big John once again got on the bus and said, "Big John doesn't pay!" the driver stood up, glared back at the passenger, and screamed, "And why not?"

With a surprised look on his face, Big John replied, "Big John has a bus pass."

Lesson: "Be sure of what is a problem in the first place before working hard to solve it."

Quite often in life, we over-evaluate problems and start working on huge solutions, spending time, money, efforts, energy and focus, whereas, in actuality, problems eventually are not that big!

So be crystal clear about what the problem is before going to solve it.

STEP 3: HAVE ENOUGH SOLUTIONS AND IDEAS

When you have understood the problem clearly and have started thinking of possible solutions, don't put any filters on the solutions. Think wildly. Think different. Think out of the box. Sometimes, a problem is just an absence of an idea.

Accept and note down all types of solutions, logical, illogical, emotional and whatever. Then, put them in hierarchy of possibility and practicality. Place the most practical and possible one on the top, and start working on it.

STEP 4: ASK EMPOWERING QUESTIONS

Another way to get different possible solutions is to ask yourself empowering questions. This will give you creativity and strength to achieve what is normally not possible. Ask Empowering Questions like:

- **What would my role model have done in this situation?**
- **What are all the possible ways to do it?**
  (easy, difficult and impossible)
- **Have I given my 100% to solve it?**
- **What is not perfect yet?**
- **Who can solve it easily? How can I take his help?**

STEP 5: BREAK PROBLEMS INTO SMALLER PARTS

By now, you have chosen the best possible solution to work upon.

Divide the tasks of this solution into 3 parts.
1) Must-do tasks (Do them immediately)
2) Should-do tasks (Do them as soon as possible)
3) Good-to-do tasks (Delegate them)

And start working on them accordingly.

STEP 6: ASK FOR HELP
Asking for help is not a sign of weakness, it's a sign of strength. Never ever hesitate to ask help from a sensible, mature and competent person.

STEP 7: PRACTISE PERSISTENCE
When a stone cutter starts hammering a big stone, he will not be able to break it in his first attempt. Sometimes, it takes 10, 20, 30 hits, and sometimes it takes 20 years to break it like Dashrath Manjhi did in Bihar (India).

Even if you break it in the 15th attempt, it does not mean the first 14 were useless. It is because of the first 14 attempts that the 15th attempt could work. So persist till the goal is achieved, and you will be able to crack nearly all the problems.

So when you believe that you can solve it, when you understand the problem accurately, think different, ask empowering questions, ask for help, practise persistence and eventually you will be able to crack nearly every problem, and that is how you will become the SUPER EMPLOYEE of your organisation.

> "One of the joys of life is finding a solution. But it's hard to ever realise this if you are resistant to having the problem in the first place."

Actionable: Make a list of all the problems you have faced, you are facing and you will be facing.

Mark a tick against the ones you have solved. I assure you, looking at the ticks will give you a more proud feeling than looking at your bank balance. Happy problem solving.

CHAPTER 9
MAGIC OF VISUALISATION

"If you can dream it, you can do it."

– Walt Disney

On October 1, 1971, on the inauguration & grand opening of Disney World, someone approached Mrs. Walt Disney and said, I wish Mr. Walt were alive to see this. His wife interrupted and said, "He did see it, that's why it's here."

What a powerful lesson this incident teaches us. In fact, all successful people have this common trait of seeing their dreams even before their actual success.

What is visualisation? Visualisation is creating a mental image of a desired future event, which you are proud of, and which gives you motivation and happiness to take action. This technique is commonly called Visualisation.

How does visualisation work scientifically? Ironically, in our childhood, when we would daydream, we were taught that it is a wrong thing. We were told to keep our eyes open and do the hard work. Now science says daydreaming along with hard work is a lethal combination. However, many people still doubt whether this visualisation thing works or not. Let me share what I have learned from science about visualisation.

This learning is from an article titled 'How to use visualisation to achieve your goals' from *Huffington Post*. According to research using brain imagery, visualisation works because neurons in our brains, those electrically excitable cells that transmit information, interpret imagery as equivalent to a real-life action. When we visualise an act, the brain generates an impulse that tells our neurons to "perform" the movement. This creates a new neural pathway — clusters of cells in our brain that work together to create memories or learned behaviours — that primes our body to act in a way consistent to what we imagined. All of this occurs without actually performing the physical activity, yet it achieves a similar result.

Who practices it? Now some of you must be wondering whether someone has really become successful by practising it. Let's put it another way. Do successful people really believe in it?

Jim Carrey shared in an interview on The Oprah Winfrey Show that he was broke and depressed when he entered Hollywood for his career in the entertainment industry. There, sitting overlooking Los Angeles, he daydreamed of success. To make himself feel better, Carrey wrote himself a cheque of 10 million $ for "acting services rendered," post-dated it 3 years and kept it in his wallet.

The cheque remained there until it deteriorated, but Carrey eventually made it when he signed the movie Dumb and Dumber.

It is one of the biggest testimonials that visualisation works. However, Jim also warns that it helps only when you are taking action and not just visualising. You cannot just visualise and go and eat a sandwich.

Let's see how some other people see visualisation:

Dr. Charles Garfield who served as Clinical Professor of Psychology in the Department of Psychiatry at the University of California School of Medicine at San Francisco (UCSF) says, "I've discovered that numerous peak performers use the skill of mental rehearsal of visualisation. They mentally run through important events before they happen."

Mark McGwire who is an American former professional baseball player says, "I study pitchers. I visualise pitches. That gives me a better chance every time I step into the box. That doesn't mean I'm going to get a hit every game, but that's one of the reasons I've come a long way as a hitter."

Megan Jendrick is an American former competition swimmer, former world record-holder, and fitness columnist. She won two gold medals at the 2000 Summer Olympics and a silver medal at the 2008 Summer Olympics. She said, "I have been visualising myself every night for the past four years standing on the podium having the gold placed around my neck."

I bet now you have no doubt that it works. But yes, don't forget it works best in synergy with hard work. So without any doubt, visualisation will help you achieve the most important goals and dreams of your life with comparatively less effort.

So after the day's hard work, before you sleep, visualise yourself as the SUPER EMPLOYEE of your organisation, visualise your work life, visualise your lifestyle, your rewards, your recognition and while dreaming all these things, just go to sleep. Now your subconscious mind will keep thinking the same things the whole night. This way, actually you are sowing seeds for your dream life, and eventually these seeds will turn into trees and bear fruits soon. So along with your hard work, keep visualising your success every day, and this will help you in unexpected ways to become the SUPER EMPLOYEE of your organisation.

> "If you want to reach a goal, you must 'see the reaching' in your own mind before you actually arrive at your goal."
>
> – Zig Ziglar

CHAPTER 10
FACE FAILURE FEARLESSLY

"I dream of a day when we will be taught in our education system that failure is a good word."

– Neeraj Bali

Unfortunately, failure is taught as a bad word in our society instead of a good word. It is taught as a backward step instead of a forward step. It is taught as the opposite of success instead of a part of success.

HOW SHOULD FAILURE ACTUALLY BE INTERPRETED?

If you ask peak performers and winners, there is no such thing as failure. For them, there are no failures. That is the only feedback mechanism.

There are no failures. That is only learning.

They are not end points. They are just turning points.

They are not obstructions. They are just instructions.

To be old and wise, you first must be young and stupid. You have to learn to fall before you can fly.

If you think successful people never feared failure, you are mistaken. In fact, they are ones who see fear of failure as a good thing. They accept it as a part of the natural process. Fear of failure should be seen as a 24 hour coach. Fear of failure keeps you on track and doesn't allow you to lose sight of your destination. As Bill Gates once said, "In business, by the time you realise you're in trouble, it's too late to save yourself. Unless you're running scared all the time, you're gone." So it's human, and it's good to carry a little feeling of fear of failure.

WHO HAS NOT FAILED?

If you think successful people never failed, you are heavily mistaken. In fact, if you look closely at the lives of all great successful people, they are actually lives of all great failures.

Walt Disney was fired from a newspaper for "lacking imagination" and "having no original ideas" and later he was turned down 302 times before he got financing for creating Disneyland.

Oprah Winfrey was demoted from her job as news anchor because she "wasn't fit for television."

Steve jobs at age 30 was left devastated and depressed after being unceremoniously removed from the company he started.

J K Rowling was famously rejected by a mighty 12 publishers before Harry Potter was accepted.

Steven Spielberg got rejected from film school… three times.

Elvis Presley got fired after his first performance.

Stephen King received 30 rejections for his first novel *Carrie*.

Col. H D Sanders (KFC) couldn't sell his chicken recipe. More than 1000 restaurants rejected him.

So remember that successful people are actually the biggest failures behind the curtain.

ADVANTAGES

Thomas J. Watson Sr., the founder of IBM, was once asked how to succeed faster. He replied, "If you want to succeed faster, you must double your rate of failure. Success lies on the far side of failure."

And sorry to say if you have not failed, you have not actually tried.

Below are 4 of my favourite quotes on failing. Whenever I am failing, facing failures, I just read them & fill myself with energy. You can find your list of thoughts on failure which gives you a positive interpretation of failure, which can give you the strength to stand up every time you fall down.

(a) "Winners are not afraid of losing. But losers are. Failure is part of the process of success. People who avoid failure also avoid success." – Robert T. Kiyosaki.
(b) Before Alice got to wonderland she had to fall.
(c) Only those who dare to fail greatly, can succeed greatly.
(d) Bigger the failure is, more glorious the victory is.

So fail forward, fail fast, fail fearlessly, and that is how you will become the SUPER EMPLOYEE of your organisation.

> "I've missed more than 9000 shots in my career. I've lost almost 300 games. 26 times, I've been trusted to take the game winning shot and missed. I've failed over and over and over again in my life. And that is why I succeed."
>
> – Michael Jordan (Ace Basketball player)

Actionable: Make a list of your failures, and one day you will proudly tell people about it on stage.

CHAPTER 11
MOST POWERFUL LAW OF SUCCESS

"All that we are is a result of what we have thought."

– Buddha

Since ages, all our religions have been teaching us the same, science has been saying it for decades, renowned people from the field of medicine, psychology, science, entrepreneurship and spirituality have said the same. We become what we think about, dream about, talk about or feel about most of the time. This is the law of attraction, which is the most powerful law of success.

Perhaps, the Law of Attraction needs no introduction. This is among one of those things which has gone viral in the last decade. Out of every 10 people who are ambitious, goal-oriented or on a mission knows about it and are practising it one way or another. It's not a new teaching. Rhonda Byrne very beautifully put all of those principles in a book named *Secret*.

This book *Secret* has sold millions of copies and a documentary is also made on this book explaining the Law of Attraction in detail. Rhonda Byrne has done a great service to mankind by writing this book. I highly recommend every dreamer to see this movie and read this book. For those who have not read it or understood the Law of Attraction, I am making a very small attempt to explain it in this chapter.

WHAT IS THE LAW OF ATTRACTION?

As per my understanding, the Law of Attraction says that everything in this universe is energy. We human beings are also energy, and energy flows wherever attention goes. Energy flows towards whatever you think and dream of most of the time. The Law of Attraction will match your Energy with that and bring it in your three-dimension reality and make your dream come true. That is why Buddha said, "All that we are is a result of what we have thought."

> "The Law of Attraction states that whatever you focus on, think about, read about, and talk about intensely, you're going to attract more of into your life."
>
> - Jack Canfield

> "Thoughts become things. If you see it in your mind, you will hold it in your hand."
>
> - Bob Proctor

- **What you think, you create.**
- **What you feel, you attract.**
- **What you imagine, you become.**

CAUTION: There are many mistakes which people unknowingly make while practising the Law of Attraction and then wonder why it is not working. I will share 3 major ones. The rest I will request you to study in detail in the book *Secret*.

Mistake 1: They choose wrong words to say right things.

Mistake 2: They use future tense.

Mistake 3: Not taking action is not an option.

Let's take an example to understand how they make this mistake.

The Law of Attraction understands and focuses on subject only and does not understand the don't part. For example, if you are consistently saying, "I don't want to be late. I don't want to be late," the law of attraction understands only the subject which is late. So guess what will happen? Most probably you will reach late. So instead of saying "I don't want to be late," delete the word don't. And instead of saying I want to (which is a future tense) use present tense. So the right sentence will be: "I have reached in time." Add some gratitude into it. "Thank GOD I have reached in time." And about mistake no. 3, I would strongly like to say, nothing will happen on its own just by thinking, feeling and visualising, YOU HAVE TO TAKE ACTION. THERE IS NO SUBSTITUTE FOR HARD WORK.

Your thoughts begin it, your emotions amplify it, and your actions increase its momentum.

So understand that our thoughts are like magnets. What we focus on, think about, stress about and worry about will manifest in our lives. Choose better thoughts and you will create a better story.

Instead of saying, "I don't want to fail," say "Thank you, GOD, for success."

Instead of saying, "I don't want to be fat," say "Thank you, GOD, for making me Slim."

Instead of saying, "I don't want to have a struggling job," say "Thank you, GOD, for giving me a happy and exciting job."

And existence at the right time will bless your dream and make it come true. This also depends upon how much better in sync you are with the Law of Attraction.

POWER OF I AM

I read this article on the Internet, and it touched my heart.

What follows "I Am?" Have you ever considered the power of the statement, "I am?" What follows these two simple words will determine what kind of life you live. "I am blessed. I am strong. I am healthy." Or, "I am slow. I am unattractive. I am stupid." The "I am's" that are coming out of your mouth will bring either success or failure. All through the day the power of "I am" is at work in our minds. Many times we use the power of "I am" against us. We don't realise how it's affecting our future.

Here's the principle. What follows the "I am" will always come looking for you. The good news is that you get to choose what follows the "I am." When you go through the day saying, "I am blessed," blessings come looking for you. "I am talented." Talent comes looking for you. You may not feel up to par but when you say, "I am healthy," Health starts heading your way. "I am strong." Strength starts tracking you down. You're inviting that into your life. Get up in the morning and invite good things into your life. Declare "I am blessed. I am strong. I am talented. I am disciplined. I am focused. I am prosperous." And always make sure God's truth follows "I am!" That's how Laws of Attraction works.

Celebrity belief in Law of Attraction: Let's hear about the Law of Attraction from people who started with a dream and despite all the odds made it possible. Do they believe in this law? You better check it…. (Source: Article by Niki Genji, manifestbetter.com.)

It's the same process I used in bodybuilding: What you do is create a vision of who you want to be — and then live that picture as if it were already true.

– **Arnold Schwarzenegger**
(Bodybuilder, Actor, Politician, and Businessman)

I would visualise having directors interested in me and people that I respected saying that "I like your work" or whatever that is. I would visualise things coming to me that I wanted or whatever, and I had nothing at that time, but it just made me feel better. At that time all it really was for me was making me feel better. I would drive home and think "well, I do have these things; they're out there and I just don't have a hold on them yet, but they're out there."

I wrote myself a check for 10 million $ for acting services rendered. I gave myself 3 years and I dated it Thanksgiving 1995. I put it in my wallet and I kept it there, and it deteriorated… But then, just before Thanksgiving 1995 I found out I was going to make 10 million $ on Dumb and Dumber.

– **Jim Carrey (Actor and Stand-Up Comedian)**

It's sort of like a mantra. You repeat it to yourself every day. "Music is my life, music is my life. The fame is inside of me, I'm going to make a number one record with number one hits." And it's not yet, it's a lie. You're saying a lie over and over and over again, and then, one day the lie is true.

– **Lady Gaga (Singer)**

Create the highest, grandest vision possible for your life, because you become what you believe.

– **Oprah Winfrey (Media Mogul, Talk Show Host, and Actress)**

The Secret is the most powerful book outside of the Bible that I have read in my life. The book is based on The Law of Attraction and how that principle – once you master it – can help you find wealth, happiness, better health, whatever you're looking for, relationships.

Like Attracts Like. You have to understand: you are a magnet. Whatever you are, that's what you draw to you. If you're negative, you're gonna draw negativity. You positive? You draw positive. You're a kind person? More people are kind to you. … If you see it in your mind, you can hold it in your hand. This is so true.

Ask. Believe. Receive. So many people overlook this simple quality. You don't have to figure it out. That's what freezes people. When you're trying to figure out your life all the way to the end, when you can't figure you out, it freezes you from trying it,' cause you go "oh I can't figure it out, oh I can't go there 'cause I don't know how." You don't have to know how! You have to ask, believe, and receive. That's as simple as it gets folks.

Gratitude is a Powerful Process. The only way to move to the next level is you must show gratitude for where you are.

If you show gratitude, it gets you to where you want to be quicker.

– **Steve Harvey (Actor, Stand-Up Comedian and Talk Show Host)**

I am no longer cursed by poverty because I took possession of my own mind and that mind has yielded me every material thing I want, and much more than I need. But this power of mind is a universal one, available to the humblest person as it is to the greatest.

– **Andrew Carnegie (Industrialist and Philanthropist)**

HOW IT WILL HELP YOU TO BECOME THE SUPER EMPLOYEE OF YOUR ORGANISATION

Choose your thoughts carefully. Choose your words carefully. Make your customised self-talk in present tense using the "I am" principle. Like my customised self-talk is:

I am the SUPER EMPLOYEE of my Organisation.

I think, speak, behave and act like the SUPER EMPLOYEE.

I am the most disciplined, accountable and hardworking employee of this Organisation.

I came early. I stay late. I take initiative. I set goals. I persist for my goals. I upgrade my skills. And that's how I have become the SUPER EMPLOYEE of this Organisation.

This is one example of self-talk. You can make your own customised self-talk.

Make your own customised self-talk. Visualise yourself being SUPER EMPLOYEE with full emotions. See yourself receiving the certificate and medal on stage from leaders of your organisation. Paste your photo on your workstation, write beautifully below it: *SUPER EMPLOYEE of the year*, and visualise yourself as the SUPER EMPLOYEE. You can get it done from a professional who can make it look like a certificate. Whenever you look at this, it will fill you with energy and passion to achieve your goal. Think, speak, behave and act like the SUPER EMPLOYEE. Fake it till you make it. And that is how you will become the SUPER EMPLOYEE of your organisation.

> "Whatever you hold in your mind on a consistent basis is exactly what you will experience in your life."
>
> – Anthony Robbins

Actionable: Get a mock certificate designed by a professional with your photo on it. Below your photo should be written: *The SUPER EMPLOYEE of the Year.* Visualise it consistently with full emotion. As a support tool, I have shared a sample of same certificate on next page.

Gratitude: I am a member of the Mastermind Group of Law of Attraction in Chandigarh City (India) in which professionals from different walks of life meet each week at a common point and discuss how the Law of attraction can help to fulfil our dreams. Indebted thanks to Mr. Rupinder who introduced me to the Mastermind Group of Law of Attraction. Thanks to Mr. Gurmeet who founded this group. Learnings from this mastermind group has blessed my life in many ways. This book is one of those blessings.

Super Employee of the Year

This Certificate is awarded to

_____

IN RECOGNITION OF YOUR EFFORT RESULTING
IN A HIGH LEVEL OF PRODUCTIVITY & PERFORMANCE

_____   _____
DATE   SIGNATURE

CHAPTER 12
MENTORING

"The number one reason people fail in life is because they listen to the wrong people and believe in that."

— Neeraj Bali

A muscular, tall and healthy man landed at a railway station carrying luggage. He went to the taxi stand and enquired from a taxi driver that he had to go to the church.

The taxi driver replied, "200 rupees, sir."

The man said, showing intelligence, that two hundred rupees for a nearby church was too much and that it seemed that the driver was cheating him. He said he could pick up his own stuff and go on his own.

The person continued carrying the luggage far enough. After a while, he saw the same taxi driver on the way. Now the man asked the taxi driver again, "Brother, now I have done more than half the distance, so how much money will you take?"

The taxi driver replied, "400 rupees, sir."

Hearing this, the man got shocked and said to the taxi driver, "First two hundred rupees was the charge, and now it's double; why is it so?"

The taxi man replied, "Sir, from that very moment you are running towards opposite side of the church, whereas the church is on the other side."

The man did not say anything and quietly sat in the taxi.

Moral: In the same way, in many parts of life, we start working directly without thinking seriously, and then ruin our hard work and time, leaving that work halfway. Before taking any work, take a thoughtful thought of what you are doing; it is part of your goal.

So mentors help us to reach our destination in less time, with less efforts, less resources and less mistakes. Better catch them as early as possible in your career and never leave them. But before that you need to understand who a mentor is.

WHO IS A MENTOR?

A mentor is someone who sees more talent and ability within you than you see in yourself and helps bring it out of you.

– Bob Proctor

He can be anyone who is mature, learned & intellectual. You can find them in any role as a mother, as a father, as a teacher, as a boss, etc. You can find them anywhere.

Mentors are like streetlights in the dark. They will not lessen the distance, they will remove darkness and show you the way, make the journey comfortable.

WHEN IS MENTORING REQUIRED?

Some people have a misconception that mentoring is required only at the initial stage of a career. However, I believe as long as you want solutions & as long as you want growth, you require mentorship. Mentors might change depending upon many things but the need for mentorship will always remain there even if you become the CEO of a company.

LET'S SEE HOW CEOs & ENTREPRENEURS VALUE MENTORSHIP

PepsiCo CEO Indra Nooyi looks for mentors in all aspects of her life: "If I hadn't had mentors, I wouldn't be here today. I'm a product of great mentoring, great coaching… Coaches or mentors are very important." She credits the mentoring she received from people around her for helping her break glass ceilings in business.

Virgin Group co-founder Richard Branson has personally benefited from a mentor-mentee relationship. Branson asked British airline entrepreneur Sir Freddie Laker for guidance during his struggle to get multinational conglomerate Virgin Atlantic off the ground. "It's always good to have a helping hand at the start. I wouldn't have got anywhere in the airline industry without the mentorship of Sir Freddie Laker," Branson has been quoted as saying.

Oprah Winfrey (Best known for her talk show The Oprah Winfrey Show) says, "Mentors are important and I don't think anybody makes it in the world without some form of mentorship," she added.

George Lucas says, "Mentors have a way of seeing more of our faults than we would like. It's the only way we grow." Now it is taking the shape of a paid industry.

Hope by now we have understood the importance of having a mentor in our career, as soon as possible.

Pray for them. Search for them. Identify them. Associate with them. Listen to them. Act on their advice. And that's how you will become the SUPER EMPLOYEE of your organisation.

> "Mentoring is a brain to pick, an ear to listen and a push in the right direction."
>
> – John. C. Crosby

CHAPTER 13
LOOK FOR STARS, NOT FOR DARKNESS

"A bad attitude is like a flat tyre. You cannot reach anywhere until you change it."

Perhaps the most read and most listened word in the field of human development & self-development is "positive attitude" and still it is also the least understood and least implemented one. If it had been implemented even by 10%, this planet would have been a better place to live in.

The meaning of positive attitude: Positive attitude does not mean only to think positive. No. That's a very small meaning of it. Positive attitude means to look for a positive even in a negative situation. Positive attitude means to interpret the positive in any situation. Positive attitude means to believe that whatever has happened has happened for a good reason.

Let me illustrate the true spirit of positive attitude through this beautiful story, which one of my friends shared with me.

A famous writer was in his study room. He picked up his pen and started writing:

Last year, I had a surgery, and my gall bladder was removed. I had to stay stuck to the bed due to this surgery for a long time.

The same year I reached the age of 60 years and had to give up my favourite job. I had spent 30 years of my life in this publishing company.

The same year I experienced the sorrow of the death of my father.

And in the same year my son failed in his medical exam because he had a car accident. He had to stay in bed at hospital with the cast on for several days. The destruction of car was another loss.

At the end he wrote: Alas! It was such bad year!!

When the writer's wife entered the room, She found her husband looking sad & lost in his thoughts. From behind his back she read what was written on the paper. She left the room silently and came back with another paper and placed it on the side of her husband's writing.

When the writer saw this paper, he found this written on it:

Last year I finally got rid of my gall bladder due to which I had spent years in pain.

I turned 60 with sound health and got retired from my job. Now I can utilise my time to write something better with more freedom, flexibility, focus & peace.

The same year my father, at the age of 95, without depending on anyone or without any critical condition met his Creator.

The same year, God blessed my son with a new life. My car was destroyed, but my son stayed alive without getting any disability.

At the end she wrote:

This year was an immense blessing of God, and it passed well!!

See!!

The same incidents but different viewpoints. The writer's wife was a perfect example of positive attitude. Otherwise, things could have been worse than that.

So next time something bad, tough or unpleasant happens, immediately ask yourself, "What's good in it?" Search for the good in it. Initially, the mind will resist. However, after 2–3 persistent attempts, your mind will show you the positive in it. If you consistently practise it, very soon it will become your second nature. And that is how you will become the SUPER EMPLOYEE of your organisation.

THINK IT OVER
German Soldier: "Sir, we are surrounded by enemies on all sides."
Adolf Hitler: "Excellent, we can attack in any direction."

> "Train your mind to see good in everything."

CHAPTER 14
INVEST IN YOURSELF CONTINUALLY

"If you are not moving up, you are moving down."

Can you tell me, among all relationships and among all loves, which should be your first love? Love for self. Unfortunately, we are taught that being selfish is bad. Well, I strongly encourage selfishness in a positive way.

WHY INVEST IN SELF?

Love to be selfish sometimes. An empty cup cannot pour anything into another cup. A sad soul cannot distribute happiness. You cannot give what you don't have inside.

So don't mind filling yourself, loving yourself and taking care of yourself. By investing in yourself, you are making yourself valuable, and the market will pay you anything. Invest in yourself first. That pays the best interest.

> "85% of your financial success is due to your personality and ability to communicate, negotiate and lead. Shockingly, only 15% is due to technical knowledge."
>
> — Dale Carnegie

Investment in self-development can be done in many ways. Some of them are

Join online courses.

Buy yourself a book.

Join the health club.

Take your mentor to lunch.

Gift yourself good wears from top of hair to tip of nail. **Founder of SUSHMA group** (the company in which I am working right now), **Mr. B.P. Mittal**, whom with due respect we all call Bade Sir, advised me a valuable lesson on dressing which I will never forget. He said, "Neeraj, invest in your clothing. Buy 2 good business suits. Your dressing affects your behaviour. You put a postman dress on a child, and he will start distributing parcels and cards at home in a playful style. You put a police dress on a child and guess what he will do. He will start firing with whatever comes in his hand. You put a doctor dress on a kid and he will take a stethoscope and start examining you."

Bade Sir beautifully explained the one beautiful side of the coin while the other beautiful side was shown by Buck Rodgers (VP Marketing, IBM) who said, "The way you dress affects the way you are perceived and the way you are perceived is the way you are treated." Work on your outer looks. (First impression helps but ultimately the real you works out.)

- **Invest in your communication skills.**
- **Invest in your self-development.**
- **Invest in your library and books.**
- **Attend seminars relevant to your industry.**
- **Attend courses to upgrade yourself.**
- **Read books to upgrade yourself.**

Listen to audio files in your car while driving to office. Your car should be your moving library.

Watch inspirational movies. Get certification of some new talent or new skill which you can quantify to management and yourself.

Be a part of some mastermind group, like I am a part of Law of Attraction Group formed by Gurmeet ji. In this mastermind group, people from different fields meet each week on a fixed date, time and place where we discuss & share our learning on how to use law of attraction to achieve our goals in life. This is an investment for my self-growth.

I overheard an audio where Earl Nightingale said, **"If you will spend one extra hour each day studying your chosen field, you will be a national expert in that field in five years or less."** Mind blowing. What a small investment and what a big reward!

So prioritise to invest in yourself mentally, physically, spiritually, financially and that over a period of few months will make you the SUPER EMPLOYEE of your organisation.

> "Formal education will make you a living.
> Self-education will make you a fortune."
>
> – Jim Rohn

Actionable: Keep a record of all investments you made in yourself for your self-growth.

CHAPTER 15
ASSOCIATION MAKES ALL THE DIFFERENCE

"You cannot change the people around you. But you can change the people that you choose to be around."

I am sure at this age you have understood why our parents always insisted on having the good company of friends wherever we are (School, College or Community) because your association will impact your thought process, which in turn will impact your behaviour, actions and ultimately your future growth.

WHAT DOES ASSOCIATION MEAN?

Association does not just mean friends. It means all those sources with whom we spend our time and which affects our thought process. This may be the books we read, movies we see and hobbies we indulge in.

Swami Vivekanand beautifully explains the importance of association in anyone's life. "The rain drop from the sky: if it is caught in hands, it is pure enough for drinking. If it falls in a gutter, its value drops so much that it can't be used even for washing the feet. If it falls on hot surface, it perishes. If it falls on lotus leaf, it shines like a pearl and finally, if it falls on oyster, it becomes a pearl. The drop is same, but its existence & worth depend on with whom it associates." So decide where you want to fall upon.

Choose your association carefully. Keep your circle small but of productive people. People on a mission. People with a purpose in life. People who are focused on their goals. Maybe people with the same habits (like reading books) or maybe with different habits. People on the same journey as you are. They may not necessarily have to be from the same company, same profession, same city but on some same common agenda.

Join some mastermind group like I joined The Law Of Attraction Group. The Law Of Attraction Group in Chandigarh has people from different age groups, different professions, different educational backgrounds but on the same mission: "Making our dreams come true using Law of Attraction."

I am also part of a community called "Positive People Positive Posts" and then a group of trainers where we share all those talks which help us to lead a successful life. You can also create a group of like-minded people from across the world, who are from the same industry or who have the same interest, where you can discuss and share all those topics which can take your professional growth to a next upper level.

Advantages: Your right association will increase learning sources, coaching and mentoring platform, and expand your network which altogether will convert into your net worth.

Jim Rohn said you are the average of 5 persons.

- **If you spend most of your time with 5 intelligent friends, you are the 6th one.**
- **If you spend most of your time with 5 brave friends, you are the 6th one.**
- **If you spend most of your time with 5 committed friends, you are the 6th one.**
- **If you spend most of your time with 5 broke friends, you are the 6th one.**
- **And if you spend most of your time with 5 SUPER EMPLOYEEs, you will be the 6th SUPER EMPLOYEE.**

These 5 SUPER EMPLOYEEs maybe from different department different company, different industry.

Being in good association is like walking in a perfume shop. Even if you don't buy one, you will radiate fragrance from your body while coming out. In one word, association means GROWTH. So associate with good friends, good colleagues, good books, good films, and that is how you will become the SUPER EMPLOYEE of your organisation.

> "You must constantly ask yourself these questions: Who am I around? What are they doing to me? What have they got me reading? What have they got me saying? Where do they have me going? What do they have me thinking? And most important, what do they have me becoming? Then ask yourself the big question: Is that okay? Your life does not get better by chance, it gets better by change."
>
> – Jim Rohn

Actionable: Slowly start creating a mastermind group in your city, with same interest and same objective. Meet once or twice a month with some progressive agenda. Read one or two good books together in a year. See 1–2 inspirational movies together, promote that group on suitable social media platform where you can invite other people of same interest across the world. Share minutes of meeting on social media platform of that community. Very soon, it will become a powerful resource and learning centre for your future growth.

CHAPTER 16
TAKE PRIDE IN YOUR WORK

"If a man is called to be a streetsweeper, he should sweep streets even as Michelangelo painted, or Beethoven composed music, or Shakespeare wrote poetry. He should sweep streets so well that all the hosts of heaven and earth will pause to say, here lived a great streetsweeper who did his job well."

— Martin Luther King Jr.

Have you heard top brass of companies such as CEOs, Presidents and Vice Presidents giving the following advice at different platforms to all aspirants for success? "Take pride in your work." Well, you might be thinking it is easy for them to say all these things when they are receiving so much perks, filthy rich lifestyle and big cheques.

But believe me, that's how they have reached there. This is one of the main reasons why they have managed to reach there. Because at initial levels of their career, irrespective of their designation and department they always took pride in their work. They believed that their work is making a difference to many. And that's how you have to proceed on your journey, if you want to reach the top.

Let me share 2 beautiful incidents from history which teaches us best about this principle.

INCIDENT 1

President John F. Kennedy was visiting NASA headquarters for the first time, in 1961. While touring the facility, he introduced himself to a janitor who was mopping the floor and asked him what he did at NASA. The janitor replied, "I'm helping put a man on the moon!" The janitor got it. He understood the vision, he was aligned with vision of company and his part in it, and he had purpose.

INCIDENT 2

On his first day in office as President, when Abraham Lincoln entered to give his inaugural address, one man stood up. He was a rich Aristocrat. He said, "Mr. Lincoln, you should not forget that your father used to make shoes for my family."

And the whole Senate laughed; they thought they had made a fool of Lincoln.

But certain people are made of a totally different mettle.

Lincoln looked at the man directly in the eye and said, "Sir, I know that my father used to make shoes for your family, and there will be many others here. Because he made shoes the way nobody else can, he was a creator. His shoes were not just shoes; he poured his whole soul into them. I want to ask you, have you any complaint? Because I know how to make shoes myself. If you have any complaint I can make you another pair of shoes. But as far as I know, nobody has ever complained about my father's shoes. He was a genius, a great creator and I am proud of my father."

The whole Senate was struck dumb.

They could not understand what kind of a man Abraham Lincoln was.

He was proud because his father did his job so well that not even a single complaint had ever been heard.

Be proud of your work.

How much pride do you take in your profession? Do you see your work as a routine chore or as a contribution to society? Do you feel that your work is making a difference to the lives of the people? How do you explain to people when someone asks you, "What do you do?"

> Do you say, "I work in a vacuum cleaner selling company?,"
> Or do you say, "I help families to live a clean and healthier life?,"

> Do you say, "I work in life insurance selling company?,"
> Or do you say, "I help people to financially secure their families and dreams of their kids and spouse when they are no more?,"

> Do you say, "I am working in a real estate company?,"
> Or do you say, "I help people take one of the most important decisions of their lives which is buying their dream home or dream office in the most ethical way?,"

When you start taking pride in your profession, when you see your work as making a difference in people's lives, then you will work with dedication and enthusiasm toward your job and then sooner or later, your work will become worship for you, and that is how you will become the SUPER EMPLOYEE of your organisation.

> "Let's not see our job as just pushing the broom,
> let's see it as, 'Helping put a man on the moon.'"
>
> – Neeraj Bali

Actionable: Make a one-line communication describing proudly what you do and how it makes a positive impact in people's lives.

I help people to……………………

CHAPTER 17
BE HONEST WITH YOUR WORK

*"Every job is the reflection of the person who did it.
Sign your work with excellence."*

Let me start this chapter with a real life incident in Japan where a strike took place in a shoe factory. Due to some conflict and disagreement between the management and employees, a strange kind of strike took place. Disagreeing employees did not stop working. They continued their work and strike in a creative way. Employees continued making left shoes only instead of a pair of shoes. After some time, when the conflict resolved, they started making right shoes also. So no wastage of time, labour and no work stopped. That's a clear example of great work attitude.

A very good point from this story is that disagreement might happen but work should not get affected. I have seen many instances in my career that sometimes conflict with senior happens and employees start giving less and less and some even stop working. Even I had also been a culprit of this mistake. But thank GOD I came out of this attitude very soon.

We should never forget that the first person who gets benefited from your sincere hard work is not your organisation but you and your family. The first person who suffers from you not giving your 100% is not your organisation but you and your family. So in any case never stop working honestly toward your organisation irrespective of how the company is reciprocating toward you.

My boss in DLF Pramerica, Mr. Atul Mandloi, used to give us repeated advice, "Even if it is the last day of yours in your organisation, work as if it is the first day. Nobody should come to know that it is your last day."

Let me share a very interesting and very empowering story which beautifully demonstrates this point. (Source: inspirationpeak.com)

An elderly carpenter was ready to retire. He told his employer-contractor of his plans to leave the house building business and live a more leisurely life with his wife enjoying his extended family.

He would miss the pay check, but he needed to retire. They could get by. The contractor was sorry to see his good worker go and asked if he could build just one more house as a personal favour. The carpenter said yes, but in time it was easy to see that his heart was not in his work. He resorted to shoddy workmanship and used inferior materials. It was an unfortunate way to end his career.

When the carpenter finished his work and the builder came to inspect the house, the contractor handed the front-door key to the carpenter. "This is your house," he said, "my gift to you."

What a shock! What a shame! If he had only known he was building his own house, he would have done it all so differently. Now he had to live in the home he had built none too well.

So it is with us. We build our lives in a distracted way, reacting rather than acting, willing to put up less than the best. At important points we do not give the job our best effort. Then with a shock we look at the situation we have created and find that we are now living in the house we have built. If we had realised that, we would have done it differently.

Think of yourself as the carpenter. Think about your house as your career. Each day you hammer a nail, place a board, or erect a wall. Build wisely. It is the only life you will ever build. Even if you live it for only one day more, that day deserves to be lived graciously and with dignity. The plaque on the wall says, "Life is a do-it-yourself project." Your life tomorrow will be the result of your attitudes and the choices you make today.

When someone asked Mahatma Gandhi, "Any message you want to leave for the coming generation," he politely said, "My life is my message." In the same way, your work should be your message. Your work should speak for you.

Work as if you are the owner of the company, respect your work, take your work as worship, and that is how you will become the SUPER EMPLOYEE of your organisation.

> "If you built a house with your work ethic, dedication & preparation, would you trust its foundation enough to live in it?"
>
> – Robert Griffin III

CHAPTER 18
YOUR GROWTH STOPPER HAS DIED

"Ninety-nine per cent of all failures come from people who have a habit of making excuses."

– George Washington Carver

What do you think is the most important factor that impacts your professional growth in your life? Is it how you were brought up, your education in school, your education in college, your city, your industry or your country? Before you answer, let me share a story with you.

STORY

One day all the employees reached the office and saw a big notice written on the door.

"Yesterday, the person who has been stopping your growth in this company passed away. You are invited to join the funeral."

In the beginning, they got sad for the death of one of their colleagues, but after a while they got curious to know who was the man who stopped their growth.

Everyone thought: *Well at least the man who stopped my progress died!*

One by one the thrilled employees got closer to the coffin, and when they looked inside they were speechless. They stood shocked in silence, as if someone had touched the deepest part of their soul. There was a mirror inside the coffin and everyone who looked inside could see himself/herself.

There was a sign next to the mirror that read:

"There is only one person who is capable to set limits to your growth... It is you. You are the only person who can influence your happiness, success and realisation."

Your life does not change when your boss, friend or company changes......your life changes when you change... you go beyond your limiting beliefs and you realise you are the only one responsible for your life.

Till the time you will keep holding someone else responsible for your rise or fall, you will never grow and the moment you start believing that whatever I am today & whatever I will be tomorrow, only I am responsible for that. That day you will start your journey toward becoming the SUPER EMPLOYEE, and that will make you SUPER EMPLOYEE one day.

> "You steadily grow into becoming your best as you choose to be accountable and accept responsibility for improvement."
>
> - Steve Shallenberger

Affirmation: My Growth is only dependent on only one person and that is me. I am responsible for my success, for my failure, for my happiness and for my grief.

SECTION B - SKILL EMPOWERMENT

CHAPTER 19

DO YOU BRUSH YOUR TEETH EVERY DAY?

"The illiterate of the 21st century will not be those who cannot read and write, but those who cannot learn, unlearn and relearn."

– Alvin Toffler

Do you brush your teeth every day? Most probably your answer is yes. Do you brush your skills every day?

If your answer is yes, good; if no, why not?

You will be paid more for your skills than for your knowledge.

Your people skills will make you valuable in the market, and your value makes you payable in the market.

One of the best sources I can recommend to you for people skills is a famous book by Dale Carnegie called *How to Win Friends and Influence People*. No book as good as it has ever been written nor will ever be written on human relationships.

At different stages in your career you will require different types of skills, and some skills will be universal, such as communication skills, which will be required at all stages in life.

As your skills grow, your designation will grow and so will your income. Don't think that learning stops after school or a college degree.

A few days ago, I read a story full of wisdom and great insight on the benefits of sharpening your skills. It was from a blog called pureinsight.org.

A young woodcutter was cutting wood in the mountains. In a short while, an old woodcutter came to work in the mountain as well. At nightfall, the young woodcutter was surprised to find out that the old woodcutter had cut more wood even though he came later. The young woodcutter made a decision secretly that he would come to work in the mountains even earlier the next morning.

The next day, the young woodcutter indeed came to work in the woods very early. He thought, "I will certainly win this time." Unexpectedly, when he carried his wood back, he found the old woodcutter had beaten him again.

On the third day, the young woodcutter decided that he would not only arrive early, but also leave late. He thought he would definitely win this time. However, the old woodcutter beat him again on that day. The same thing happened on the fourth and fifth day.

On the sixth day, the young woodcutter could no longer stand it and raised the question to the old woodcutter, "I start working earlier than you and stop working later than you. How come you beat me every time? Besides, I'm also younger than you."

"Alas, young man!" The old woodcutter patted him on his shoulder and said, "After I get home every day, the first thing I do is to sharpen my axe. While you are sleeping your fatigue off, your axe is getting duller and duller. Therefore, even though I am older than you, start working later than you, and leave earlier than you, my axe is sharper than yours. A tree will fall after I chop five times, but only after you chop more than ten times." The young woodcutter understood completely.

The old saying says, "An artisan must first sharpen his tools if he is to do his work well." If one wants to do his job well, he must first sharpen his tools. If a student wants to get a good score, he must first enrich his knowledge. If a company wants to increase its share of the market, it must first be well organised internally. If a person wants to obtain others' respect and attention, he must first behave well.

The young woodcutter was only paying attention to the results but ignoring the axe- sharpening factor of the process. That is why he only got half the results with double the effort. However, the old woodcutter enriched his own self, which is the key to success!

Abraham Lincoln said, "Give me six hours to chop down a tree and I will spend the first four sharpening the axe."

Now let me ask you, "When was the last time you sharpened your axe?"

SHARPENING YOUR AXE CAN BE DONE IN DIFFERENT WAYS

Sharpening the axe is an activity. You too can sharpen the axe of your life. Here are examples of axe-sharpening activities:

Read a book every day.

Join a gym; do aerobics, yoga or meditation.

Pick up a new hobby. Stretch yourself physically, mentally or emotionally.

Overcome a specific fear you have or quit a bad habit.

Identify your area of improvements. Understand, acknowledge and address them.

Ask for feedback and get a mentor.

85% of your financial success is due to your personality and ability to communicate, negotiate and lead. Shockingly, only 15% is due to technical knowledge. (From Carnegie Institute of Technology)

Consciously polish your skills every day like you brush your teeth every day.

- **Polish your problem-solving skills.**
- **Polish your people skills.**
- **Polish your communication skills.**
- **Polish your technical skills.**
- **Polish your managing skills.**
- **Polish your decision-making skills.**

This will make you one among the most valuable resources in your organisation, in your industry and in the market place, and that is how you will become the SUPER EMPLOYEE of your organisation.

> "Take advantage of every opportunity to practice your communication skills so that when important occasions arise, you will have the gift, the style, the sharpness, the clarity, and the emotions to affect other people."
>
> - Jim Rohn

Actionable: Choose one skill every month/every quarter on which you will focus, and focus on that skill only.

CHAPTER 20
NOT CHANGING IS NOT AN OPTION

"When you're finished changing, you're finished."

– Benjamin Franklin

Perhaps the best answer to "why do you need to change?" can be given by an article titled *The changing face of competition that can knock you down* by Mr. Rajesh Srivastava, who is a corporate consultant, entrepreneur and academic.

I have summarised the key points from that article and request you to read an unabridged version of this article, which is available at foundingfuel.com.

Till recently, competition was visible and direct. Car manufacturers competed with other car manufacturers and at best with makers of other four-wheelers like jeeps, or two-wheelers. In most cases, competition was benign—a company would get ample opportunity to respond and recover.

That is no longer the case. Competition has become invisible, indirect and lethal. Nokia, Motorola and BlackBerry are cases in point—they lost ground to Apple, a "cross-industry" competitor.

Cross-industry competitors are powered by technology—they can come from anywhere and deliver knockout punches—as seen in the following sectors:

Banking: Traditional banks will face stiff competition from these cross-industry competitors which are acting as payment gateways for money transfer like Paytm.

Taxis: The decades-old industry is facing survival issues across the world since the advent of taxi aggregators, spearheaded by Uber. Uber started with 4 wheeler taxi services and now in India they are providing 2 wheeler services also. No surprise, they will start offering air taxi soon, providing competition to charter air services.

Coca-Cola and McDonald's, which are considered to be the strongest brands, are now worried because of changing emerging trends in consumer behaviour. Though both are tasty, they are now perceived as harmful to health, and who is gaining from this changing trend of consumer behaviour? You guessed it right. It's Subway which promises fresh and healthy food.

Gillette is another example of shifting trends threatening competitive advantage. For decades it has dominated the men's shaving market globally by offering "the best a man can get," investing heavily in research and development and non-stop innovation. Today it finds a challenge in the form of a global fashion trend that has young men sporting a stubble or a beard.

Winston Churchill once said: "A lie gets halfway around the world before the truth has a chance to get its pants on."

Diet Coke seems to be at the receiving end of this insight. An Internet rumour that has gone viral holds aspartame, an ingredient, to be carcinogenic. Most diet colas, including Diet Coke, contain aspartame. Result: Millennials, who are constantly on the Internet, are exposed to this rumour and are shunning Diet Coke.

That brings us to a new source of competition—rumours.

What should your response be when faced with these indirect, invisible and lethal sources of competition?

Remember, these New Age competitors are versatile and strike you when you least expect it.

Are there any other strategies to take on this new hydra-headed competition? Indeed there is. Be open to change. It involves becoming your own fiercest competitor and disrupting and destroying your own business to emerge in a more formidable avatar.

Has any company followed such a strategy? Several have, including Wikipedia, YouTube, Netflix and Gillette.

Every few years, Gillette launches a razor that makes the earlier version redundant. It started with a single-blade safety razor, then launched a double-blade razor, followed it up with a three-blade razor and now its Fusion Razor has five blades.

If the disrupt and destroy strategy sounds too "violent," another strategic path is to buy out competition. That is what Facebook did to an emerging competitor, WhatsApp.

Thanks to Mr. Rajesh Srivastava who wrote this article.

So the crux I interpret from this article is, "Be ready to change, or else you will be thrown out of the market by this indirect, invisible & lethal competition."

Best testimony of this principle by a very successful company: During the press conference to announce NOKIA being acquired by Microsoft, Nokia CEO ended his speech saying this, "We didn't do anything wrong, but somehow, we lost." Upon saying that, all his management team, himself included, teared up sadly.

Nokia has been a respectable company. They didn't do anything wrong in their business, however, the world changed too fast. Their opponents were too powerful.

They missed out on learning, they missed out on changing, and thus they lost the opportunity at hand to make it big. Not only did they miss the opportunity to earn big money, they lost their chance of survival.

The message of this story is, if you don't change, you shall be removed from the competition. So you need to change yourself.

Someone rightly said:
- **People who will change before time will lead.**
- **People who will change with changing time will succeed.**
- **People who will change after changing time will be extinct.**

So if you want to lead in your organisation or industry, not only do you need to change with time, I suggest you to try to foresee what the future requirements of your industry will be. What type of knowledge will be required? What types of skills will be required? What can the possible trends in the coming time be in your industry?

Change with those skills which can help you to lead. Change with that knowledge that can help you to lead. Change with those habits which can help you to lead. Change with that discipline which can help you to succeed at present and possibly lead in coming times, and that is how you will become the SUPER EMPLOYEE of your organisation.

> "Your success in life isn't based on your ability to simply change. It is based on your ability to change faster than your competition, customers, and business."
>
> – Mark Sanborn

Actionable: Find out one change in yourself which if done can take your career growth to the next level. Set it as a goal and work on it.

CHAPTER 21
ASK YOURSELF EMPOWERING QUESTIONS

"It's not the answer that enlightens. It's the question."

All the greatest discoveries and progress that have taken place have come up as a result of asking empowering questions and as a result of challenging the status quo.

Newton asked, "Why do apples fall down every time? Why don't they go up?" and he discovered gravity which later on unfolded many other secrets of the world of science and benefited man in many ways.

The Wright brothers asked, "Why can't we fly like birds?" and they invented the aeroplane.

Someone might have thought why do we have to depend on petrol only for running cars and other vehicles? And today we have companies which are making electric cars.

Someone might have thought why go to banks for financial transactions? And we have mobile banking today.

It does not matter what question you ask, what matters is *how* you ask a question.

One of my biggest learning in my career and biggest help in my career came at a stage when I was in depression, and I was reading a book by Anthony Robbins. This book changed my life and put the confidence back in me. I highly recommend everyone to read this book, *Awaken the Giant Within*, as soon as possible in your career for fast growth.

Particularly Chapter 8: 'Questions are Answers' provided me the way out to come out of every challenge. I am sharing the enlightening story shared by Anthony Robbins through which he very beautifully showed that it does not matter what question you ask, what matters is how you ask a question. This is the story of the escape of a prisoner from a Nazi camp, which was an impossible task. Let's see how he did it, in the words of Anthony Robbins.

They needed no reason. They came simply because he was of Jewish descent. The Nazis stormed into his home, arresting him and his entire family. Soon they were herded like cattle, packed into a train, and then sent to a death camp in Krakow. His most disturbing nightmares could never have prepared him for seeing his family shot before his very eyes. How could he live through the horror of seeing his child's clothing on another because his son was now dead as the result of a "shower?" Somehow he continued.

One day he looked at the nightmare around him and confronted an inescapable truth: if he stayed there even one more day, he would surely die. He made a decision that he must escape and that escape must happen immediately! He knew not how, he simply knew he must.

For weeks he'd asked the other prisoners, "How can we escape this horrible place?" The answers he received seemed always to be the same: "Don't be a fool," they said, "there is no escape! Asking such questions will only torture your soul. Just work hard and pray you survive."

But he couldn't accept this—he wouldn't accept it. He became obsessed with escape, and even when his answers didn't make any sense, he kept asking over and over again, "How can I do it? There must be a way. How can I get out of here healthy, alive, today?"

It is said that if you ask, you shall receive. And for some reason, on this day, he got his answer. Perhaps it was the intensity with which he asked his question, or maybe it was his sense of certainty that "now is the time." Or possibly it was just the impact of continually focusing on the answer to one burning question. For whatever reason, the giant power of the human mind and spirit awakened in this man. The answer came to him through an unlikely source: the sickening smell of decaying human flesh.

There, only a few feet from his work, he saw a huge pile of bodies that had been shovelled into the back of a truck—men, women, and children who had been gassed. The gold fillings had been pulled from their teeth; everything that they owned—any jewellery—even their clothing, had been taken.

Instead of asking, "How could the Nazis be so despicable, so destructive? How could God make something so evil? Why has God done this to me?," Stanislavsky Lech asked a different question. He asked, "How can I use this to escape?" And instantly he got his answer.

As the end of the day neared and the work party headed back into the barracks, Lech ducked behind the truck. In a heartbeat, he ripped off his clothes and dove naked into the pile of bodies while no one was looking. He pretended that he was dead, remaining totally still even though later he was almost crushed as more and more bodies were heaped on top of him.

The fetid smell of rotting flesh, the rigid remains of the dead surrounded him everywhere. He waited and waited, hoping that no one would notice the one living body in that pile of death, hoping that sooner or later the truck would drive off.

Finally, he heard the sound of the engine starting. He felt the truck shudder. And in that moment, he felt a stirring of hope as he lay among the dead. Eventually, he felt the truck lurch to a stop, and then it dumped its ghastly cargo—dozens of the dead and one man pretending to be one of them—in a giant open grave outside the camp.

Lech remained there for hours until nightfall. When he finally felt certain no one was there, he extracted himself from the mountain of cadavers, and he ran naked twenty-five miles to freedom.

What was the difference between Stanislavsky Lech and so many others who perished in the concentration camps? While, of course, there were many factors, one critical difference was that he asked a different question. He asked persistently, he asked with expectation of receiving an answer, and his brain came up with a solution that saved his life. The questions he asked himself that day in Krakow caused him to make split-second decisions that led to actions that significantly impacted his destiny.

But before he could get the answer, make the decisions, and take those actions, he had to ask himself the right questions.

Anthony Robbins shared another two good examples on the power of asking right questions in an article in *Fortune*

Magazine, where he was sharing excerpts of his book: *Money: Master the Game.*

He shared that we've all heard, the maxim: "Ask and you shall receive!" But if you ask better questions, you'll get better answers! It's the common denominator of all highly successful people. Bill Gates didn't ask, "How do I build the best software in the world?" He asked, "How can I create the intelligence [the operating system] that will control all computers?" This distinction is one core reason why Microsoft became not just a successful software company but also the dominant force in computing— still controlling nearly 90% of the world's personal computer market! However, Gates was slow to master the web because his focus was on what was inside the computer, but the "Google Boys," Larry Page and Sergey Brin, asked, "How do we organise the entire world's information and make it accessible and useful?" As a result, they focused on an even more powerful force in technology, life, and business. And which resulted into Google.

I am sure by now you have understood that asking smart questions will provide you smart answers and asking stupid questions will provide you stupid answers.

So ask yourself empowering questions in the right way.

How can I take my company ahead in the next 1 week?

What extra am I offering?

What value am I adding to the company?

What is one thing which no one can do better than me in this department, in this region, in this company as a whole?

What do I need to learn the most to get promoted to the next level?

What is the one thing which if I inculcate in myself can double my productivity?

What can I improve?

What do I need to change?

What more can I do?

How much better can I become?

How much harder can I train?

Never ask, "Can I do it?" The brain will always say NO because we are programmed like that since childhood. Ask "How can I do it?" Initially the brain will resist because of past programming, however, when you consistently ask this, the brain will start coming up with answers one by one, and you will end up with so many answers to that challenge.

So whenever you are given some challenging task to do, don't ask yourself, "Can I do it?" Ask, "How can I do it?" You will start coming up with solutions then.

Ask intelligent questions. Ask empowering questions. Ask creative questions. Work hard on them, and that is how you will become the SUPER EMPLOYEE of your organisation.

> "Questions are the Answers."
>
> - Anthony Robbins

CHAPTER 22
LEARN PEOPLE SKILLS

"85% of your financial success is due to your personality and ability to communicate, negotiate and lead. Shockingly, only 15% is due to technical knowledge."

– Carnegie Institute of Technology

This chapter is dedicated to the legend Dale Carnegie who wrote the all-time bestseller book *How to Win Friends and Influence People*. No book on human skills has ever been written so beautifully and perhaps can never be written in the future also.

WHY SHOULD YOU READ THIS BOOK?

One of the first people in American business to be paid a salary of over a million dollars a year (when there was no income tax and a person earning 50 dollars a week was considered well off) was Charles Schwab. He had been picked by Andrew Carnegie to become the first president of the newly-formed United States Steel Company in 1921, when Schwab was only 38 years old.

Why did Andrew Carnegie pay a million dollars a year, or more than three thousand dollars a day (in 1921) to Charles Schwab? Why? Because Schwab was a genius? NO. Because he knew more about the manufacture of steel than other people? Nonsense. Charles Schwab told Dale Carnegie that he had many men working for him who knew more about the manufacture of steel than he did.

Schwab says he was paid this salary largely because of his ABILITY TO DEAL WITH PEOPLE.

This book can put you on the same path.

This book will teach you the most simple, the most important yet most ignored and least followed human relationship principles in the most beautiful way via real life examples.

This book has 10 sections dedicated to the importance and development of different types of people skills of utmost importance for your growth.

You will learn why not to do the most common mistake in human history: the tendency to criticise. This small mistake alone kills 80% of our resources. Our relations.

You will learn to touch the most desired human urge of every human being around you – "the desire to be important" by giving sincere and honest appreciation. And if you can master this skill, you will have an army of people around you to help and support you.

You will learn the benefits of listening, calling someone by his name and talking in terms of the other person's interest.

You will learn the best of communication skills and leadership skills.

You will learn the most difficult skills in the easiest way to get people to start thinking in your way.

You will learn how to remove worry and tension from your life and make your life happier by focusing on the controllable.

You will learn the subtle art of making someone realise his own mistake in the most skilful and comfortable way.

It will make you a better human being by teaching you the most difficult skill to acquire and that is "admitting your mistake." It will teach you sympathy. It will teach you to start looking at things from others' perspective, which solves 70% of our problems and conflicts.

You will learn:

The magic of asking questions instead of giving orders

The magic of slightest improvement

On a lighter note, I always say that if I become the prime minister of this country, I will make this book compulsory after a certain age in the whole education system so that this world will become a beautiful place to live in.

This book changed my life. From a boy with an inferiority complex, who could not talk to even one stranger in my childhood to a Professional Training career where I have spoken to thousands of strangers. This book changed me from being a people-scared person to becoming a people-addicted person. From a people- repelling person to a people-attracting person.

This book is your gateway to become the SUPER EMPLOYEE of your organisation if you can learn and apply the skills taught in this book. Period.

Actionable: Start reading and acting on Dale Carnegie's book. Put it on your Kindle.

CHAPTER 23
BE A GREAT NETWORKER

*"If you want to go fast, go alone.
If you want to go far, go with others."*

– African proverb

WHAT IS NETWORKING?

Networking in my eyes means how well connected you are in society, inside and outside your social and professional circle.

If you are a veteran, then networking is a platform to share and contribute back to the society. If you are a new entrant then networking is a platform to learn from veterans with a promise that one day you will come here on this platform and contribute back and be a guide & mentor to the new entrants again.

Networking should not be seen only as a hunting ground but as a cultivation platform. Cultivation of relations, cultivation of ideas, cultivation of talents.

Networking can be of two types: Intra-Networking which means networking within the company and Inter-Networking which means networking within the industry. Both are necessary for our career growth.

BENEFITS OF INTER-NETWORKING

When you are well connected to the people outside your organisation (and within your industry) you get many benefits like knowing who the top performer in your industry in your city is, and sometimes from their mouth we come to know who the best is in the country. What are the good practices adopted by them? How are they different from others? What are their strategies? What is the future of the industry? How do other companies handle the challenges you are facing? Who are best pay masters?

Answers to all these questions open the path to your professional growth.

BENEFITS OF INTRA-NETWORKING

When you are well connected with selected people inside your organisation, in different departments and at different levels, it has the following benefits.

Many of them by virtue of their experience understand the company culture better. They can guide you about growth in the company better than anyone else.

They are in the best position to tell what company is looking for the next leadership post or the next promotional candidate.

They are in the best position to tell what to avoid.

They are in the best position to tell how they achieved the growth in the company. They are in the best position to tell where you are prone to make mistakes. These selected ones will coach and mentor to you.

They may not necessarily be in the same department or in the same hierarchy. Example: If you are in sales, having a good relationship with HR seniors or sales seniors will always help.

Connect with people who are going where you are going.

Everything you want in life is just one man away. And that one man is somewhere in your network.

HOW TO GET NETWORKED

Do volunteer in company initiatives whether CSR (Corporate Social Responsibility) programmes or EXPO or Conferences.

Remember birthdays and give people pleasant surprises.

Appreciate their knowledge, skills and achievements wherever possible.

Find out 2–3 top performers in every competitor company. Gradually, as opportunity serves, call them and appreciate their stature and their success. Build a relation. Call them for lunch/dinner. Build a friendship with them.

When you network with industry leaders, game changers and consistent performers, your resources will grow manifold. Your network will become your net worth. Hang out with the people who are on the same mission as you are. Hang out with the people who are much smarter than you, and that is how you will become the SUPER EMPLOYEE of your organisation.

> "Everything you want in life is just one man away. And that one man is somewhere in your network."

CHAPTER 24

LEARN ONE NEW SKILL EACH YEAR

"Journey of thousand miles begins with a single step."

– Lao Tzu

The world never remembers the ordinary ones and hardly forgets the extraordinary ones. So how do you become the extraordinary one? Well one of the ways to become extraordinary is to walk an extra mile. Extra mile in terms of learning, doing and contributing.

Here in this chapter, I will be talking about going an extra mile in terms of learning. Learning one new skill each year. Commit yourself to learn and master one new skill each year like public speaking, calligraphy, Excel, PowerPoint, digital marketing, etc. The list is long. Learn whatever benefits you in your professional growth. The EXTRA will make you valuable in the marketplace.

Moreover, Science also says, "When you learn new skills, your brain gets strong, with higher brain functioning which boost your intelligence & success. Perhaps the brain is the only organ which grows with its usage. More you use it, more you challenge it, more it grows.

However we tend to ignore this by giving the excuse of time availability. If you say you have shortage of time, I won't argue but suggest you take baby steps. Take baby steps, as baby as 15 minutes a day. Fifteen minutes a day for a year. Now you might think what difference can 15 minutes a day make? Well I used to think the same till I heard Jim Cathcart on Ted Talks. Jim Cathcart was living an ordinary life till he heard one single line message from Earl Nightingale on a radio station. This line, this message changed his destiny from an ordinary government clerk to a national expert influencing thousands of lives. This video changed my life with an amazing lesson hidden in it. Let's read what million dollar message Jim Cathcart heard from Earl Nightingale. I have tried to note it down word by word.

THE TRANSCRIPTION IS GIVEN BELOW

Jim Says, 'See, I never expected to be anything but ordinary. I was raised to be nice and ordinary. I expected I would grow up to be, like dad worked for the phone company. I figured I'd go to work for the phone company, maybe work in an office. I figured I'd work till 65 and I'd have kids, I'd retire at 65 and then I'd die at statistical average age for my gene pool. That's what I expected. Until one day in 1972 on the radio in the next room to mine, I heard a voice that changed everything.

I was working for the Little Rock Housing Authority, Little Rock Arkansas, urban renewal agency. I was a government clerk making $525 a month. I weighed 200 pounds. I smoked 2 packs of cigarettes a day. I never set a goal in my life. I didn't have a college degree and no money in the bank. I was newly married with a new baby at home, and I didn't expect much from life.

And in the next room, I heard the voice of Earl Nightingale, known at the time as the dean of personal motivation. He was on 900 radio stations around the world, and what he said that day will forever resonate with me. He said, **"If you will spend one extra hour each day studying your chosen field, you'll be a national expert in that field in five years or less." That hit me like a tornado; 'it rearranged everything in my life.'**

Jim says, 'I started doing the math, an hour extra a day, say five days a week, 50 weeks a year, that's 1250 hours over five years. If I spend, me just ordinary me, 1250 hours studying one subject, wow! I could actually be a national expert. What I want to be an expert at? It was not urban renewal. And then it occurred to me a few weeks later, I want to do what that guy on the radio's doing. But I had no idea what that was. I just knew it felt right to get into the field of human development. I thought we'll see, an hour a day, I am a government clerk. I've got eight hours a day. I could do this by Thursday.

And then I started thinking about what he'd said and I took him seriously, an hour a day. I focused; well I thought I was kind of behind the game, so I needed two hours, and three and four and five. So I over compensated and I became fanatical about the field of human development. And in that five year period I went from being a government clerk with very little aspiration to being a full-time speaker and trainer. In two years, that was 1972; in 1974 I started buying Earl Nightingale's training materials and selling them to businesses.

By 1984, his company was selling my training materials worldwide. They sold $3.5 million worth of one of my first audio albums. In the first two years it was out. I was blown away.

His formula works, and I've seen it work for hundreds and even thousands of people in the many many years since that time that I've been sharing that message.'

So I am sure now if 1 hour can make you a national expert in your chosen field, at least 30 minutes a day can make you at least a company expert in 1–2 years. People in your organisation should see you as the second Google of that subject. In case the Internet is not working and they cannot access Google, the next alternative as guidance that should come to their mind is your name.

So start your journey, find out the niche where you want to be the best and which can take your professional growth to the next level. Discipline yourself to spend 30 minutes each day in learning that skill and in one year, you will probably be the company expert in that domain. And do it next year and next year and next year, and that is how you will become the SUPER EMPLOYEE of your organisation.

> "Baby steps count, as long as you are going forward.
> You add them all up, and one day you look back and you'll be surprised at where you might get to."
>
> – Chris Gardner

CHAPTER 25
LEVERAGE TECHNOLOGY TO INCREASE PRODUCTIVITY

"Technology is helping companies to become super companies, ideas to become super ideas and man to become superman."

– Neeraj Bali

DID WE KNOW?

Uber, the world's largest taxi company owns no vehicles.

Facebook, the world's most popular media creates no content.

Alibaba, the most valuable retailer has no inventory.

Airbnb, the world's largest accommodation provider owns no real estate.

Apple, with sales of over 200 million smart phones and tablets does not own a factory.

WhatsApp, with 3 Billion messages a day does not own servers.

- Oyo Rooms - Country's largest chain of Affordable Hotel rooms does not own any hotel.

These were the companies which were started by 1st gen entrepreneurs who combined an idea with technology and became such big companies in just 6–7 years which other companies took 40–50–60 years to reach. And all this has been made possible because of technology.

What will you think of me if I say I don't even know how to make an account on any social site or for that matter I don't know how to make a Gmail account? What will you think of me? I still take help from my colleagues to open an account in social sites.

Now what if I say there is hardly any day when I don't use apps like Evernote, Pocket or Feedly on my IPad or mobile and use them for an hour for the last 7 years? By the way, have you heard of these apps? What… you don't know? Now what should I think about you? Giggles…

Actually I am obsessed with these 3 apps and the credit for making me learn these apps goes to my cousin Vineet Sharma from Dehradun (India) who is a tech guy. Seeing my interest he suggested these 3 apps, approximately 10 years ago and since then I am using them nearly every day. If I had not known about Evernote, Pocket and Feedly, I would most probably not have been able to write this book or write it in 10 years. Thank you, Vineet. This was a great gift from your side.

So what have you learned from the above two examples? Technology is helping companies to become super companies, ideas to become super ideas and man to become superman. And surely it is also helping employees to become SUPER EMPLOYEES.

So adapt and learn productive technology in your work style which can sharpen your skills & increase your networking, productivity & expertise manifold. That's how you will progress on your journey to become the SUPER EMPLOYEE of your organisation.

> "Technology is a gift of GOD. After the gift of life, it is perhaps the greatest of God's gifts. It is a mother of civilisations, of arts and of sciences."
>
> – Freeman Dyson

CHAPTER 26
LEARN TO BE GOOD AT SELLING

"Life is a series of sales situations."

In a good portion of my initial career, I used to hate sales. I used to think sales was all about misselling & shrewdness. I thought it was not for good people and kind-hearted people.

Now I laugh at myself. How wrong was I? Now I repent why I came so late into sales. I was lucky enough to come out of this misconception. Still many people will keep thinking like how I earlier used to think. They will still feel the same way. This is not for me. They will still feel that I cannot do it. Let's see what sales actually is & why you think you cannot do it. Let's understand what sales is.

- **Sales is a belief in your product or idea.**
- **Sales is an effective presentation.**
- **Sales is an effective communication.**
- **Sales is asking the right questions.**
- **Sales is true counselling.**
- **Sales is helping people to take a right decision.**
- **Sales is follow up.**
- **Sales is handling objections.**
- **Sales is good service and doing homework.**

Which among the above mentioned things is one which you cannot do or cannot learn, or most importantly, which of the above things are you not doing already?

Irrespective of your profession or department, you are already doing it. Only the degree matters.

EXAMPLES

Let me share some good news. Whether you like it or not, you are already doing sales. Consciously or unconsciously, you are doing it. Directly or indirectly, you are doing it. When you are convincing your son why he should complete his homework and then go play, you are selling him the importance of doing homework first.

- **When you are convincing your boss for 5 days leave, you are in sales.**
- **When you are convincing HR for good increment, you are in sales.**
- **When you are convincing your landlord to not increase rent, you are in sales.**
- **When an entrepreneur convinces to put money in his idea, he is selling.**
- **When a professor is teaching, he is selling his knowledge.**
- **When a surgeon is operating, he is selling his skills.**
- **When a singer is singing, he is selling his voice.**
- **When a prime minister of a country goes to another country and shows them the benefit of investing in his country, he is selling.**

So from Peon to Prime minister of the country, we are all in sales. Nothing ever happens unless someone sells something to somebody.

I am not saying you have to join sales; I am saying you have to learn this growth boosting skill consciously which will help you to grow in your career, personal life and social life exponentially. Commit to read at least one sales book every year. It will fill your life with confidence, happiness and high self-image. So learn effective communication, learn effective presentation, learn handling objections and learn persuasion, and people will walk on the path, which you will show them, and that is how you will become the SUPER EMPLOYEE of your organisation.

> "Everything in life is a sale and everything you want is a commission."
>
> – Grant Cardone

CHAPTER 27
NEVER SAY NO

"If someone offers you an amazing opportunity and you are not sure you can do it, say yes - then learn how to do it later."

– Sir Richard Branson

Though I always encourage, "Learn to say No," however, I also encourage at some places to NEVER SAY NO.* Instead say, "LET ME TRY." So what's the difference?

When I say, "Learn to say NO," it means NO to unproductive tasks, unplanned tasks and non-contributing tasks.

When I say, "Never say NO," it means don't say no to an opportunity. If you develop this trait in yourself, it will increase your brand value, your skills, your confidence and confidence of people dealing with you.

My mentor, Mr. Deepak, who is my elder brother, always shares his experience of his work in a photographic lab in New York. Some customers used to come to him with certain jobs which they had tried everywhere and which had been refused.

Then they used to come to Mr. Deepak.

And Mr. Deepak would never say, "I can't do it." He always said, "Let me try." And he says that has taught him many great things. In the words of Mr. Deepak, "I never said NO to my important clients even if I knew they have already tried this work at other places and after not being satisfied they are trying with me. So I know they are mentally prepared to hear NO. Then why not take a chance and say, "Let me try?" Even if you fail in delivering the required result, your "let me try" attitude instead of directly saying NO will make you different from the crowd and the other person will appreciate it."

Advantages of never saying NO *: These YES can be an opportunity to showcase your talent, can be an opportunity to increase your market value, can be an opportunity to bring you in the limelight and can be an opportunity to take you to the next level.

Bollywood actor Aamir Khan said a dialogue in the film *Dhoom,* "Jo kam duniya ko namumkin lage, wahi mauka hota hain kartab dikhane ka." ("The work which seems impossible to the world is also the opportunity to showcase your talent.")

So when you start resisting saying NO, when you start seeing the hidden opportunity in NO and when you start working on them with full passion, you will be on your way to become the SUPER EMPLOYEE of your organisation.

> "If you are looking for big opportunity, find out a big problem."

CHAPTER 28
BECOME MORE VALUABLE

"Those who seek a better life must first become a better person."
– Jim Rohn

Everything you want, you get and you don't get from your professional career revolves around 3 words: BECOME MORE VALUABLE. That is what I learned from Jim Rohn. Thanks to legend Jim Rohn, who was among the pioneers of the self-help field.

The answers to all our professional grudges & professional disappointments lie in these 3 words. BECOME MORE VALUABLE.

Let's look at some of the most common complaints and solutions we have in our career.

Complaint 1: My organisation does not pay me well.
Solution: Become more valuable.

Complaint 2: My organisation does not give me promotion.
Solution: Become more valuable.

Complaint 3: My organisation does not give me facilities.
Solution: Become more valuable.

Complaint 4: My colleagues don't treat me well.
Solution: Become more valuable.

Make yourself valuable to the place called MARKETPLACE. It does not matter how experienced you are, what matters is how much value you bring to the table consistently. Now I don't need to tell you how you are going to make yourself valuable. The Internet is full of such information, and you better know what all you need to do to become valuable in your organisation. All I can say is that if you are determined enough to increase your value, people will run after you to pay unlimitedly for your skills, talents and gifts. Let me share a real life experience on that.

Let's learn *How I can increase my own value* from the life of Michael Jordan. Michael Jordan was born in 1963, in the slums of Brooklyn, New York.

He had four siblings and his father's earnings were not sufficient to provide for the whole family.

He grew up in a poor neighbourhood. Exposed to mindless violence and heavy discrimination in the slums, he saw for himself only a hopeless future.

His father saw in Michael, a lost soul and decided to do something.

He gave Michael, who was 13 years old, a piece of used clothing and asked: "What do you think the value of this outfit would be?"

Jordan replied, "Maybe one dollar."

His father asked, "Can you sell it for two dollars? If you can sell it, it would mean that you are a big help to your family."

Jordan nodded his head, "I'll try, but no guarantee that I'll be successful."

Jordan carefully washed the cloth clean. Because they didn't have an iron, to smoothen the cloth, he levelled it with a clothes brush on a flat board, then kept it in the sun to dry. The next day, he brought the clothes to a crowded underground station. After offering it for more than six hours, Jordan finally managed to sell it for $2.

He took the two dollar bill and ran home.

After that, every day he looked for used clothing, washed and ironed it, and sold it in the crowd.

More than ten days later, his father again gave him a piece of used clothing, "Can you think of a way you can sell this for 20 bucks?"

Aghast, Jordan said, "How is it possible? This outfit can only fetch two dollars at the most."

His father replied, "Why don't you try it first? There might be a way." After breaking his head for a few hours, finally, Jordan got an idea.

He asked for a cousin's help to paint a picture of Donald Duck and Mickey Mouse on the garment. Then he tried to sell it in the school where the children of the rich study.

Soon a housekeeper, who was there to pick his master, bought that outfit for his master. The master was a little boy of only 10 years. He loved it so much that he gave a five dollar tip. 25 dollars was a huge amount for Jordan, the equivalent of a month's salary of his father.

When he got home, his father gave him yet another piece of used clothing, "Are you able to resell it at a price of 200 dollars?" Jordan's eyes lit up.

This time, Jordan accepted the clothes without the slightest doubt. Two months later, a popular movie actress from the movie *Charlie's Angels*, Farah Fawcett, came to New York for her movie promos. After the press conference, Jordan made his way through the security forces to reach the side of Farah Fawcett and requested her autograph on the piece of clothing. When Fawcett saw this innocent child asking for her autograph, she gladly signed it.

Jordan was shouting very excitedly, "This is a jersey signed by Miss Farah Fawcett, the selling price is 200 dollars!" He auctioned off the clothes to a businessman for a price of 1,200 dollars!

Upon returning home, his father broke into tears and said, "I am amazed that you did it, my child! You're really great!"

That night, Jordan slept alongside his father. His father said, "Son, in your experience selling these three pieces of clothing, what did you learn about success?"

Jordan replied, "Where there's a will, there's a way."

His father nodded his head, then shook his head, "What you say is not entirely wrong! But that was not my intention. I just wanted to show you that if a piece of used clothing which is worth only a dollar can also be increased in value, then how about us - living & thinking humans? We may be darker and poorer, but what if we CAN increase our VALUE?"

This thought enlightened young Jordan. Even a piece of used clothing could be made dignified, then why not me? There is absolutely no reason to underestimate myself.

From then on, Michael Jordan felt that his future would be beautiful and full of hope. He went on to become the greatest basketball player of all times.

So here is the mantra again, "Become more valuable." Become so valuable that your organisation would like to retain you for whole life and would go to a good extent to retain you. Read more books. Stay with people smarter than you. Network intelligently. Come early. Go late. Work on yourself, your skills, your knowledge, your gifts, and become nearly indispensable. That's how you will become the SUPER EMPLOYEE of your organisation.

> "Never wish life were easier, wish that you were better."
> – Jim Rohn (Business Philosopher)

SECTION C - ACTION EMPOWERMENT

CHAPTER 29
BE THE FIRST ONE TO DO IT

*"Every task is a self-portrait of the person who did it.
Sign your work with excellence."*

Can you name the first person to land on the moon?
Can you name the first person to climb Mount Everest? Chances are high that a good percentage of people will be able to answer it.

And who was the 2nd person to land on the moon?

Who was the second person to climb Mount Everest? Chances are high that very less percentage will be able to answer it, even if I gave you options.

And the reason is obvious. People remember the first ones.

Likewise, whenever your senior gives you some task, it may be asking a question to a group or delegating a task to a team. I suggest that you try to be the 1st one to reply and try to be the first one to complete it. Be the first one to do it before the deadline. Every time you do it, you will create an image of yourself in the mind of your senior that you are the most sincere future leader, future manager and next guy to be promoted.

But be sure to check the priority list. Just to be the number 1 respondent, don't start working on priority no. 10 instead of no. 1. It is not a wise decision. If as per priority hierarchy, it is not important to do, keep your boss in the loop that you are already working on something of higher importance, and ask for some more time to reply. That will help you to be differentiated from others and give you an edge in your career growth.

So if it does not hit your priority list, try to be a volunteer, try to be no. 1 in responding, try to be no. 1 in taking action, try to be no. 1 in completing, and that is how you will become the SUPER EMPLOYEE of your organisation.

CHAPTER 30
BE FOCUSED ON YOUR KRAs

"You cannot hit a goal you cannot see."

Sometimes we live under the wrong notion of being a great employee, most hardworking, most wanted, but it does not pay in the end. For example, when I joined the corporate world in the 1st year as Training Manager, I did everything. In fact, in my own eyes, I did the best. Good praise. Hard work. But at the year end, I got a very small raise. Then after counselling, I came to know that all my efforts were in the direction different to the assigned KRAs (Key Responsibility Areas).

My boss Abul Hashim taught me, "Bali, there are 3 types of things: Must-do things, should-do things, good-to-do things. You are hired for must do things whereas you are spending your time and energy on rest of the two. You are being hired to achieve your KRAs. The rest is just distraction."

Your growth is directly proportional to the achievement of your KRAs, and achievement is possible only when you are focused on your KRAs.

Abul Sir used to remind us again and again two pieces of wisdom to stay focused:

"Out of sight out of mind."

"Clearer the goal nearer the goal." And it has helped us a lot.

I share this example quite often. Let's say your doctor advises you to drink 4 litres of water in a day. Now if you keep this in mind and remember it orally, chances are very high that you will hit nearly 40% of your target. And if you keep a water bottle on your work station and at any prominent place where you spend your maximum time, chances are very high that you will hit 80% of your target. It is only because out of sight becomes out of mind.

Likewise paste your KRAs on your work station. This way, you will be keeping a regular eye on KRAs and tracking progress monthly on it. At the end of the year, at the time of annual review, you will not be surprised with what happened regarding your increment and promotion. If you are regularly tracking it, you will always be aware of what you deserve and what you will get. If your KRAs are not in your mind and are before your eyes, then you will not get a surprise shock at the end.

Plan your day's schedule as per your KRAs. If your daily schedule does not include activities which are your KRAs, then you are perhaps going in a direction, which will not give you a raise, promotion or recognition in your career. So work hard and work smart.

Paste your KRAs on your work station, plan your day as per your KRAs, remain focused on them and persist till you achieve them, and that is how you will become the SUPER EMPLOYEE of your organisation.

> "Your main competitors are not others in your industry. Your main competitors are distractions. Don't let them beat you - stay focused."
>
> – Darren Hardy

CHAPTER 31
ALL DO IT SOME. SOME DO IT ALL.

"Many of life's failures are people who did not realise how close they were to success when they gave up."

- Thomas Edison

"You all are good starters, but poor finishers. But remember you will be acknowledged for what you finished and not for what you begin." This is one of the strong messages given by our boss Mr. Abul Hashim to the Training team of HDFC Standard Life.

Now I realise what a great message that is.

Most of us start a job with excitement, passion and hard work but don't maintain the consistency till the end. We leave the task in-between. And that separates men from boys.

All does not mean everything.

When I say some do it all, I mean there are very few people who when they start a task, they do it till end, not 50%, not 60%, not 70%, but complete 100%.

Immediately don't say yes to every task. Check your priority list and time available. If it does not fit in your priority list, try to delegate it. Extend the time line. Dare to say NO gently.

If it fits in priority list, take the suitable time limit for completing it. But once you have given your words to somebody, be sure to complete it within that time frame. There lies an opportunity to build your brand. Your image should be such that if you have said ok to a job, it means it is completed come what may.

So give your words carefully and once given do everything to keep your word. Be a good starter and a great finisher, and that is how you will become the SUPER EMPLOYEE of your organisation.

> **"Arise awake and stop not till goal is achieved."**

CHAPTER 32
DARE TO ACCEPT RESPONSIBILITY

"Avoiding responsibility is avoiding growth."

– Neeraj Bali

I was watching a famous Hollywood blockbuster film which has the quote, "With great power comes great responsibility." Yes, you guessed it right. The film is Spider-Man. How apt it is. If you are looking for a bigger designation, bigger ranks, more power in your career, then you must be prepared to take bigger responsibility also.

One of the best definitions of Responsibility is:

A duty or obligation to satisfactorily perform or complete a task (assigned by someone, or created by one's own promise or circumstances) that one must fulfil, and which has a consequent penalty for failure.

It is said that if you want to check someone for his character, give him Power. Likewise if you want to judge your employee for his readiness for the next leadership role, assign him a responsibility and see how he reacts.

Think how a boss will feel if any of his employee goes to him and says, "Sir, I understand you have many roles to perform, many goals to achieve and many tasks to fulfil. I will be happier and thankful if you can delegate some of the tasks to me so that you can concentrate on the most important one."

Taking responsibility is helping someone but above all at first it is helping yourself. Taking responsibility means sharing the burden of your seniors, taking the load off shoulders from seniors. More responsibility means more trust created.

THERE CAN BE 4 LEVELS OF RESPONSIBILITY ACCEPTANCE

Level 1: You go to your boss and volunteer and ask, "Boss give me some more responsibility," and your boss will think, "Man, this guy is on road for next level."

Level 2: When boss asks the team who will do it, and you are the first person to take that responsibility.

Level 3: Responsibility given to you only and you accept it despite doubts whether you will be able to do it. So you don't say NO to your senior.

Level 4: Responsibility is given to you and you avoid it by making some excuse.

So move ahead, buddy. Cross your fears of failure. Have a spine, and go to your boss and say to him, "Boss, give me some more responsibility," and that is how you will become the SUPER EMPLOYEE of your organisation.

> "The more you take responsibility for your past and present, the more you are able to create the future you seek."
> – Unknown

CHAPTER 33
LET'S EMBRACE RISKS

"The biggest risk is not taking any risk. In a world that's changing really quickly, the only strategy that is guaranteed to fail is not taking risks."

– Mark Zuckerberg

I read on the Internet the story of Xerox's research company PARC, who invented the personal computer probably 7 years before but did not take the risk in commercialising it and scaling it. Apple got the inspiration from them and built it, took the risk and sold personal computers (Lisa and Macnitosh) and left Xerox way behind.

Risk should always mean calculated risk and not a blind one.

For a growth seeking person, not taking risk is not an alternative. Here comes in the formula of my boss, Abul Hashim, which he used to remind us time and again and the formula is "TINA." TINA means THERE IS NO ALTERNATIVE. If you want progress, growth, legacy, you have to take the risk. There is no alternative.

Overcoming fear and taking risk has to be an inseparable part of success journey. If you will not take risk, you will always be a part of the crowd but never be on stage. If you will not take risk, you will always remain a follower, but never be a leader.

If you will not take risk, you will always remain a bogie, but never be an engine.

You have to overcome the fear of taking risk. George Addair very rightly said, "Everything you've ever wanted is on the other side of fear." Risk cannot be eliminated, but it can certainly be reduced.

How you can reduce this fear of risk:

Take a little spiritual path:

Listen to your gut feeling, believe that you are taking this risk for a better cause and GOD will help you, and accept that there will be discomfort along with.

Steve jobs in his advice full of wisdom and spirituality said, "You can't connect the dots looking forward; you can only connect them looking backwards. So you have to trust that the dots will somehow connect in your future. You have to trust in something–your gut, destiny, life, karma, whatever. This approach has never let me down, and it has made all the difference in my life."

Take baby steps: Our brain is scared of taking a leap immediately. So that's why baby steps are recommended. Our brain gives us the permission to take baby steps and with that we can slowly and slowly get courage to take bigger steps. Don't forget, big shots are actually the small shots who keep on shooting.

How I overcome my fear of taking risk: Whenever I am afraid of taking risk, I read some of my favourite quotes on risk taking which pumps me and fills my heart with courage and my brain with wisdom. It's actually like taking a shot of liquor, which gives you a kick (on the lighter side). I am sharing some of my favourite quotes said by achievers:

> To dare is to lose one's footing momentarily.
> To not dare is to lose oneself.
>
> – Søren Kierkegaard

> Progress always involves risks. You can't steal second base and keep your foot on first.
>
> – Frederick B. Wilcox

> This nation was built by men who took risks — pioneers who were not afraid of the wilderness, business men who were not afraid of failure, scientists who were not afraid of the truth, thinkers who were not afraid of progress, dreamers who were not afraid of action.
>
> – Brooks Atkinson

> Only those who dare to fail greatly can ever achieve greatly.
>
> – Robert F. Kennedy

> We fail more often by timidity than by over-daring.
>
> – David Grayson

> I really don't think life is about the I-could-have-beens. Life is only about the I- tried-to-do. I don't mind the failure but I can't imagine that I'd forgive myself if I didn't try.
>
> – Nikki Giovanni

> **Whenever you see a successful business, someone once made a courageous decision.**
>
> – Peter F. Drucker

> **Man cannot discover new oceans unless he has the courage to lose sight of the shore.**
>
> – Andre Gide

> **Do one thing every day that scares you.**
>
> – Mary Schmich

> **Leap and the net will appear.**
>
> – Zen saying

These thoughts fill my brain and heart with a purpose and energy that helps me to take next bold step. Maybe it can help you too.

Since Thomas Edison took the risk of putting his whole life's saving and earning into the discovery of the light bulb after refusal of banks and experts, we have light bulbs and electricity today.

Since Steve job, Michelle Dell and Mark Zuckerberg took the risk of leaving their studies in between and focusing on their startups, we have companies like Apple, Dell and Facebook today.

Since Jeff Bezos, Narayan Murthy and Shiv Nadar took the risk of leaving their jobs, we have companies like Amazon, Infosys and HCL today.

Since Tom Monaghan, Walt Disney, Ray Kroc risked all their earnings for the sake of their dreams, we have companies like Domino's Pizza, Disney World and McDonald's with us today.

Likewise, if you take a risk today for a good cause, only then you will become the SUPER EMPLOYEE of your organisation tomorrow.

> "Often the difference between a successful man and a failure is not one's better abilities or ideas, but the courage that one has to bet on his ideas, to take a calculated risk, and to act."
>
> – Maxwell Maltz

Actionable: Every day, among 10 goals, set 1 or 2 such goals that you are scared of doing because they look like risks, and do it despite all fears.

CHAPTER 34
ASK FOR HELP

"Asking for help is not a sign of weakness. It's a sign of wisdom."

A young girl and her father were walking along a forest path. At some point, they came across a large tree branch on the ground in front of them. The girl asked her father, "If I try, do you think I could move that branch?"

Her father replied, "I am sure you can, if you use all your strength."

The girl tried her best to lift or push the branch, but she was not strong enough and she couldn't move it.

She said, with disappointment, "You were wrong, dad. I can't move it." "Try again with all your strength," replied her father.

Again, the girl tried hard to push the branch. She struggled but it did not move.

"Dad, I cannot do it," said the girl.

Finally her father said, "Young lady, I advised you to use 'all your strength.' You didn't ask for my help."

MORAL

Our real strength lies not in independence, but in interdependence. You will not find any individual person who has all the strengths, all the resources and all the stamina required for the complete blossoming of their vision.

To ask for help and support when we need it is not a sign of weakness, it is a sign of wisdom.

I read somewhere that in the Disney World Company, there is a concept called Idea Wall. Every employee has to write an idea about overcoming the present challenge the company is facing. Then they collectively get a lot of ideas to overcome that challenge. And then they start working on the best idea till the problem is resolved. This is also another form of asking for help. If such a big company can ask for help, why not you and me?

All great work done – is done by a team. Where everyone offers their help in the form of their gifted talent, whether composing a song or launching a space ship. Don't try to do everything by yourself.

Appreciate that everyone has some kind of strengths and compliment them for that. Instead of wasting your time to learn that skill, why not ask their help in that particular area? What's the harm in asking for help?

All NGOs ask for help.

All corporates ask for help.

All governments ask for help from neighbouring countries for their expertise.

All entrepreneurs ask for help in terms of funding.

Go to anyone whom you appreciate for a particular skill. Never hesitate. Say "I appreciate your talent, and I need your help in this capacity." He will also feel happy. And that army of resources, skills and talents will be available to you. Asking for help will make you a right person to overcome any challenge and to achieve any goal.

That is how you will become the SUPER EMPLOYEE of your organisation.

> "You can do anything. But not everything."
>
> – David Allen

CHAPTER 35
BE KNOWN FOR YOUR WORK CULTURE

"Your work is to discover your work and then with all your heart to give yourself to it."

— Buddha

In some places, perfection is a habit not an attitude!

I read somewhere, the American Computer Giant IBM decided to have some parts manufactured in Japan as a trial. In the specifications, they set a standard that they would accept only three defective pieces per 10,000 pieces. When the delivery came to IBM, there was a letter accompanying it.

We, Japanese people, had a hard time understanding North American business practices. But the three defective parts per 10,000 pieces have been separately manufactured and have been included in the consignment in a separate package mentioned – "Defective pieces as required, not for use."

In this world, the Japanese are known for punctuality.

Americans are known for their enterprising spirit. In corporate, Apple is known for challenging the status quo.

Honda is known for reliability.

In my office, Neeraj is known for handwriting.

Neha is known for being the most aggressive sales manager.

Jagmeet is known for punctuality.

What are you known for? What is one quality you are remembered for? Or what is one quality for which you want to be remembered for?

- **Are you preparing yourself for a common quality?**
- **Are you preparing yourself for no quality?**
- **Are you preparing yourself for an extraordinary quality?**

If your answer is the 3rd one, you are preparing yourself to become the SUPER EMPLOYEE of your organisation.

> "Your personal brand is a promise to your clients... a promise of quality, consistency, competency, and reliability."
>
> – Jason Hartman

CHAPTER 36
CAN YOU SEE YOUR MISTAKES?

"The highest form of intelligence is to observe yourself without judgement."

Let me share an example of the most proactive review ever done. This is the story of a child who went to a store and rang up on phone a lady. (Store owner was listening.)

Child said, "I will mow your lawn."

Voice from other side, "Already have a person who is doing it."

Child said, "I will additionally wash the car also once in a month."

Voice from other side: "No."

Child said, "I will do it at 10 $ less per month."

"No." the reply came, and lady on the other side put the phone down. Shopkeeper felt pity on the child and said, "I will like to offer you the job."

"No, I do not need it. I already have the job. I am the same boy who works at her home. I was just checking if I am replaceable and if she is happy with my services."

Perhaps this is one of the best reviews that happened anywhere. I am sure there is no need to tell what this story teaches us.

Self-review is very important. To look at yourself in a neutral way is the greatest insight.

To see and accept the faults in yourself is the greatest courage. It is very difficult to do self-surgery. But if you can do that, that's the greatest courage and greatest wisdom. And if you can do that consistently & impartially, you will be on your way to become the SUPER EMPLOYEE of your organisation.

> "The most fundamental aggression to ourselves, the most fundamental harm we can do to ourselves, is to remain ignorant by not having the courage and the respect to look at ourselves honestly and gently."
>
> – Pema Chodron

CHAPTER 37
HOW BADLY DO YOU KNOW YOUR PRODUCT?

"There are no experts, only varying degrees of ignorance."

– Amit Trivedi

One of my very good friends in the Real Estate industry is Neeraj Kumar. I learned one very good thing from him. Hold on to the subject. You give him Rs. 500, he will tell you the weakness of the product which you probably have not heard of. Now if you give him Rs. 1000, he will convert most of the weaknesses into strengths, which you again probably have not heard of. That was the kind of confidence and grip he was having on every aspect of his product or subject.

On 23rd September 2016, I listened to an audio by an army officer during an army convocation. It was on the culture of Indian army, values, overcoming religion boundaries, etc. Very Impressive and patriotism-evoking. Then, a few days later, my first cousin Lt. Col. Rajneesh came to our place. During conversation, I thought of sharing the audio with him. I asked casually, "Brother, have you listened to that audio by an army officer on patriotism?"

He interrupted me in-between by asking, "The one which is 7 min 11 sec?" and I was blank. I just could not understand what he said. Then after 2–3 seconds, I understood what he said and I said, "I don't know." As the mobile was in my hand and audio clip was right there on screen, I just checked the time length of the audio, and I was amazed. It was ditto 7 minutes 11 seconds. That's the grip you need to have on your profession. That is what I call how badly you know your product, your profession, your subject.

There are two things. First, my brother caught the message before I completed my sentence and second he was exactly aware of the time length of the audio. What to talk next? What to ask next? Then I assumed that he must have heard it many times.

That exactly happens in our professional encounters; if you answer the first 2–3 questions very confidently and accurately, the person asking you questions then assumes from the accurateness of your answer that you have command over your subject. You know what he is asking about and the rest of the job becomes easy.

Work so hard on your product or subject that everyone should think of you when they don't get the answer. Learn something new every day. Be the pre-Google of your subject.

Read something new about your subject. Learn something new every day about your subject. Be the first one to know about coming changes in your industry. Be the Google of your subject, and that is how you will become the SUPER EMPLOYEE of your organisation.

> "Never become so much of an expert that you stop gaining expertise. View life as a continuous learning experience."
> – Denis Waitley

CHAPTER 38
BE A CONTINUOUS "WORK IN PROGRESS"

"Continuous improvement is better than delayed perfection."

— Mark Twain

I read somewhere….

Let's take a quick look at the format of the high jump event. Every competitor gets three tries to clear the bar, and if they can do that they get to take another shot after the bar is raised. If they can't clear it in three tries, they get knocked out. The elimination continues till there are fewer people left after each round — until there are three — then two — and finally one — the winner. Does it stop there? No it doesn't. Even after the winner has been identified, the bar gets raised again and the winner jumps to see if he can clear the bar. If he succeeds, the bar gets raised again

— and again — until such time as he tries and fails after three attempts. The high jump is also about seeing how high the finest athlete can jump. And it's an event where the winner has to fail — before he wins.

Winning in high jump — and indeed in business and in life — is not just about being better than the other guy. It's about going beyond, and testing yourself to see how good you can be.

It's a good mind-set to adopt. A mind-set that urges you — nay compels you — to strive for excellence.

John Buchanan — the two-time World Cup winning Australian coach built his all- conquering team on a philosophy of "Good is not enough if better is possible." The truly great leaders get comfortable with failure. A loss is never the end of the world. Being a leader is simple really. Just think like a high jumper! Keep your eyes on the hurdle, on the challenge ahead. Believe in your ability to jump over the bar, to overcome. After every success, raise the bar. And yes, one more thing. Remember. You haven't really won until you've failed…!.

And that should be your attitude towards your work. Constantly raising benchmarks. Constantly upgrading. Constantly sharpening. Constantly stretching. Constantly learning, and that is how you will become the SUPER EMPLOYEE of your organisation.

> **"Let your life be a continuous work in progress."**

CHAPTER 39
ARE YOU PREPARING FOR THE NEXT LEVEL?

"When opportunity comes, it is too late to prepare."

– John Wooden

Till 36 years of age, I had remained inquisitive to one question and that was, "How do you become lucky in your career?" I read many books, listened to many wise people, went to many astrologers and attended many self-development seminars till I listened to one right answer which I never understood at that time. And that was, 'Luck is what happens when preparation meets opportunity.' Great answer, but I didn't understand at that time.

But now after having read, observed and stayed with many successful people, I think I better understand it. Let me share an example to illustrate this:

In 1994, Jack Ma heard about the Internet. In early 1995, he went to the US and with his friends they helped him get introduced to the Internet. During his first encounter he searched the word "beer." Although he found information related to beer from many countries, he was surprised to find none from China. Further, he tried to search for general information about China and again was surprised to find none. At that point, Jack Ma understood the power of Internet and opportunity in terms of missing Internet services in the world's biggest country. He prepared for this opportunity, capitalised at the right time and made himself lucky. Today, Jack Ma is the founder and executive chairman of Alibaba Group, a conglomerate of Internet-based businesses. This is what I say, "Luck is what happens when preparation meets opportunity."

When I ask my team mates if they are prepared for the task, and they say they are fairly prepared, and rest, they will see what happens, I advise them, **"It is better to be prepared and not get a chance rather than getting a chance and not be prepared."** I give them my personal example. When I joined real estate, I was in non-sales department, always willing to join sales, which was not happening. But I kept my knowledge, presentation and script updated in the hope of getting a chance someday. I was always learning on how to be great at selling. And then one fine day, a situation came where we were short of sales managers, and I was temporarily put in that role for some time to cover up till new ones came.

I was prepared, so everything went well. With God's grace, I made good sales and eventually earned good incentives, got promotion after some time and got team leadership profile eventually. All this would not have happened if I had not done my pre-preparation.

Always try to understand what kind of qualities, skill and knowledge is required at the next promotional post. Take the help of your seniors.

Ask your seniors how they will rate you on a scale of 1–10 scale on parameters which are required at the next level. You do your own rating also. After going through both these ratings, give yourself a genuine rating on these parameters, and you will get feedback. You will find a gap & start working on it gradually.

Preparation is the key to confidence. The more prepared you are, the more confident you will be and the lesser anxiety you will face. **The separation is in the preparation. What separates men from boys is preparation.** And now finally at this stage of my life, I have understood it well that thorough preparation will make you lucky. And that's how everyone becomes lucky. And that's how you will become lucky. And that is how you will become the SUPER EMPLOYEE of your organisation.

> "By failing to prepare, you are preparing to fail."
> – Benjamin Franklin

SECTION D - DISCIPLINE EMPOWERMENT

CHAPTER 40
NEVER START YOUR DAY UNLESS...

Either you run the day or the day runs you.

- Jim Rohn

One of the most important productivity habit you can develop is planning your day on paper. Yes, on paper. Yes, you read it right, on paper. First of all, most of us, I would say nearly 80% of us, don't do this at all. We just act like courier boys: reach office, pick up the task given or take the task that comes our way and start working on it. No brain applied. No pre-planning done.

Some of you will be happy to tell me that you are not among those 80%. They plan it but not on paper, in mind only. So let me put you in the 15%. People who are little better than those who have no plan. Keep in mind... a little better only because what is in mind skips out of mind and what gets written gets done.

Now comes the class. Only 5% of people do it religiously on paper, and they are the people sooner or later who are bound to be among the best performers and most wanted ones of the companies.

Now honestly ask yourself where you stand.
- **In category of 80% employees?**
- **In category of 15% employees?**
- **In category of 5% employees?**

This is one discipline which you need to practise at every stage of your career. In fact, the more badly you want success, the more religiously you have to follow this habit. All CEOs, all business leaders, all peak performers follow this habit religiously because they understand that their every minute is worth thousands of dollars. So how can they come unplanned? No way.

My brother and my mentor, Mr. Deepak, often advises me, "Neeraj, if you can wake up at 5 am and have a day planned on paper, you are bound to be successful in life and if you cannot develop this habit, you are bound to remain average or might be below average throughout your career."

Advantages: If we talk about advantages of this habit, then none better than Brian Tracy to explain it. Brian said, "Every minute you spend in planning saves 10 minutes in execution. This gives you a 1000 per cent return on Energy."

In addition to this, planning your day on paper keeps you in control, gives you happiness, increases your confidence, projects you as a thorough professional and keeps you focused on the most important tasks.

Disadvantages: Whereas if we talk about disadvantages of not planning your day on paper, then none better than Jim Rohn to explain it. Jim Rohn said, "If you don't design your life plan, you will fall into someone else's life plan and guess what they have planned for you. Not much."

In addition to this, you will always feel like you're not in control. If you will not work on your priority list, someone will make you work on his priority list.

Best time to plan: Best time to plan today was yesterday night because the whole night the subconscious mind keeps working on it and second best time is early morning.

Accidentally a few months back, I read a productivity tip by CEO Jack Groetzinger of a company called SeatGeek. And to my surprise, I was following it for more than 9 years.

Jack Said, "I keep a do-list of everything I want to do. In addition to sort of listing everything out, I also rank everything by importance and put next to it an estimated number of minutes that I think it will take to complete. I have a start and end time associated with each of those as well, so it sort of gamifies the process of working through your to-do list." Believe me, the day I don't come with a written and prioritised day plan in office, my productivity goes down.

First you make habits then habits make you. So make a strong habit that you will never start your day unless you have planned it on paper. That way you will be focused, in control, respecting time, and that is how you will become the SUPER EMPLOYEE of your organisation.

> "Every minute you spend in planning saves 10 minutes in execution. This gives you a 1000 percent return on Energy."
> – Brian Tracy

Actionable: Never ever start your day unless you have put it on paper.

CHAPTER 41
FOCUS ON PRIORITIES

"The key is not to prioritise what's on your schedule, but to schedule your priorities."

- Stephen Covey

Have you ever felt that you are overburdened, over occupied and have less time in the day? Probably all of us have felt this. Time and tasks are not the real problem. The real problem is not planning, not prioritising and probably not learning time management. So this chapter will help us on that front.

Sometimes we carry a wrong picture of working hard. I am a hard worker. I am always busy. But we don't realise what we are busy with. Busy with what, in succeeding or remaining stagnant? Busy remaining an expert or remaining average? Busy with a top priority or least priority job? The world measures us by productivity & action instead of intent.

There can be many ways of focusing your priorities also. Real Estate Super Woman and Shark Tank Star Barbara Corcoran advises, "The best way to approach your day, when you are arriving at your desk and may be you have 50 things on your TO DO LIST that you planned a night before and you have limited 8 hours or 12 hours if you are really working hard, is to go through your list ruthlessly and label every single item as A, B or C. I do that every morning.

A is something that is gonna push your business ahead, getting closer to your goal line, also A are urgent things that must be done. Quick things that must be done.

After that you have B's.

B's are things which are gonna help you being more productive, help you get your business ahead.

And C's are all the nice things you really want to do, the easy stuff.

The only thing that is important is to focus on A's that are very important and B's that are secondary important. You can have your C's go on to tomorrows TO DO LIST and next day's TO DO LIST. My C's travel for 2 years. I really wanted to do them but I did not have time, so I focus on my A's & B's. You don't have enough time. You never have enough time. So you have to focus on what is going to make a difference." (Source: Inc Video.)

One of the best things I learned from my seniors & bosses on time management and prioritisation is the "Art of prioritising quadrant." You can divide all tasks in the four quadrants.

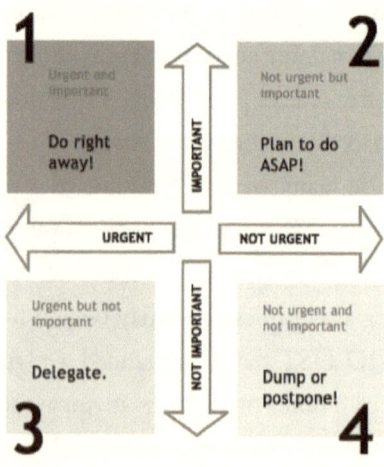

In Quadrant 1 (High Priority Quadrant) those tasks will come which are of high importance and high urgency. You have to work on them immediately.

In Quadrant 2 (Medium Priority Quadrant) those tasks will come which are of high importance and low urgency. You have to schedule quality and uninterrupted time to complete this. Preferably you have to complete them in the same day.

In Quadrant 3 (Low Priority Quadrant) those tasks will come which are of low importance and high urgency. So you can reschedule them or delegate them.

In Quadrant 4 (No Priority Quadrant) those tasks will come which are of low importance and low urgency. You can do them later and don't have to worry about them at this moment. You can postpone them to the next day.

With this in mind and in practise, your productivity level will increase manifold.

So you can follow any of the above two or you can follow and design your own, but remember to remain focused on top priorities.

Be organised so that you are in control. Put your day plan on paper. Remain focused on high priority jobs. Learn to delegate. Learn to say NO politely. Remain disciplined. First things first. It will help you to achieve your daily, weekly, monthly goals, and that is how you will become the SUPER EMPLOYEE of your organisation.

> "Many things are not equal but everyone gets the same 24 hours a day, 7 day a week. We make time for what we truly want."

Actionable: Remain focused on your high priority tasks in your Everyday TO DO LIST.

CHAPTER 42
LEARN TO SAY NO EVERY DAY. PERIOD.

"Half of the troubles of this life can be traced to saying yes too quickly and not saying no soon enough."

— Josh billing

Often times we get derailed from our schedule because somebody requests us to do something, which was not in our schedule, and we don't have the ability or guts to say NO to them, and the whole schedule gets disturbed. Now you are on an unplanned thing from a planned schedule. Now you are on a less priority job from a high priority job just because you couldn't say NO to that person for any reason.

NO is the smallest, bitterest and scariest word in this existence. Fear of word NO has stopped many dreamers from achieving their dreams, stopped many persons from getting their dream life partners and stopped many entrepreneurs from working on their dream projects.

But if you will never learn to start saying NO, you will never become the SUPER EMPLOYEE.

So let's learn how to say NO gently, respectfully and skilfully.

Step 1: How I do it: Whenever some sudden unplanned task or unexpected Request comes to me, I immediately say Give me some time or at least 10 min to think about it. I will get back to you. In this period, I Decide what to take on.

Unexpected request vs planned priority. And then reframe my NO in decent way.

Step 2: Start with Yes & Say YES before NO.
Saying NO in a decent way means you have to say it in such a way that the other person does not feel hurt. His concern is also taken care of while you can continue working on your genuine prioritised task.

Example: Let's say you have an appointment with a doctor for your mother's checkup and your boss assigns you a task at the same time

Say to your boss politely, "I would love to do it right now, however, if you permit me, I want to share that I have already taken an appointment from the doctor to get my mother checked, and after that I will immediately work on it and get it delivered to you by 9 pm. Is it feasible?"

Share the genuine reason not a fake one or else it will harm your reputation. People will respect you eventually for your straightforwardness.

Step 3: Acknowledge them & appreciate them for understanding your position and adjusting.

Step 4: Find out some way to do that task if it is possible to do it right at that time by delegating it to someone or else make sure that the job gets done later on after your priority work is done. Get back to him.

- **Learn to say NO gently & genuinely.**
- **Learn to say NO politely.**
- **Learn to say NO skillfully.**

And this will help you to remain focused on your top priorities, and that is how you will become the SUPER EMPLOYEE of your organisation.

> "You can be a good person with a kind heart and still say no."
> — Lori Deschene

CHAPTER 43
MOST POWERFUL HABIT FOR PRODUCTIVITY

"Leaders are readers but not necessarily all readers become leaders."

One of the most important and most common habits among all leaders and super successful people is that they have a habit of reading. They still have a great thirst for learning. They never think that they are already at peak. They never think that they cannot learn anything by reading books.

Leaders of one industry are learning from leaders of another industry. For them, there is no point after which they stop learning and keep making them better and better and better. And that's why, perhaps, they are super successful because they keep learning and put that learning into action.

Bill Gates read about Warren Buffet perhaps to learn how to spot opportunities and capitalise from them.

Warren Buffet, perhaps, read about Jeff Bezos on how Amazon is shrinking the world and moving toward becoming no. 1 company in the world.

And Jeff Bezos, perhaps, read about Elon Musk and Richard Branson who are thinking about the next horizon called space.

The easiest way to learn from the super successful is to read the books written by them and on them.

I was reading an article written by Andrew Merle in Observer.com where he beautifully compiled the reading habits of super successful leaders in various industries. Here is what I learned about reading habits of super successful people.

Bill Gates reads about 50 books per year which means approximately 1 book per week.

Mark Zuckerberg resolved to read a book every 2 weeks throughout 2015.

Oprah Winfrey selects one of her favourite books every month for her book club members to read and discuss.

Elon Musk is an avid reader and when asked how he learned to build rockets, he said, "I read books."

Mark Cuban reads more than 3 hours every day.

Warren Buffet was once asked about the key to success, and he pointed to a stack of nearby books and said, "Read 500 pages like this every day. That's how knowledge works. It builds up, like compound interest. All of you can do it, but I guarantee not many of you will do it." Buffett takes this habit to the extreme—he read between 600 and 1000 pages per day when he was beginning his investing career, and still devotes about 80% of each day to reading.

A study of 1200 wealthy people found that they all have reading as a pastime in common.

But successful people don't just read anything. They are highly selective about what they read, opting to be educated over being entertained. They believe that books are a gateway to learning and knowledge.

In fact, there is a notable difference between the reading habits of the wealthy and the not-so-wealthy. According to Tom Corley, author of Rich Habits: The Daily Success Habits of Wealthy Individuals, rich people (annual income of $160,000 or more and a liquid net worth of $3.2 million-plus) read for self-improvement, education, and success. Whereas poor people (annual income of $35,000 or less and a liquid net worth of $5,000 or less) read primarily to be entertained.

Successful people tend to choose educational books and publications over novels, tabloids and magazines. And in particular they obsess over biographies and autobiographies of other successful people for guidance and inspiration.

If reading as a pathway to success isn't enough to get you motivated, consider these health benefits of reading: Reading has been shown to help prevent stress, depression and dementia, while enhancing confidence, empathy, decision-making, and overall life satisfaction.

In my transformation from a boy with an inferiority complex to a confident dreamer, reading self-help books, reading autobiographies of successful people and successful entrepreneurs played a big role. After some time, I made a big mistake in my career. I stopped reading books thinking that I knew enough to make a good career or may be could not discipline myself for this powerful habit. And that's where my career took a dip. I made this mistake and urge you all not to make it. Let reading good books written by or written on super successful people be your consistent and committed habit.

So read about industry leaders, super successful super sales performers, game changers, successful CEOs and successful entrepreneurs. Learn from them. Put those learnings into action, and that is how you will become the SUPER EMPLOYEE of your organisation.

> **"TODAY A READER. TOMORROW A LEADER."**

Actionable: Make sure you read at least one book every month.

CHAPTER 44
DO MONTHLY REVIEW WITH YOUR BOSS

"Feedback is the breakfast of champions."

– Ken Blanchard

Formula of success has changed from time to time, and it will keep on happening like that. This was a constant reminder from my boss Mr. Sandeep Punj. Some elements plus. Some elements minus. Some elements universal.

In old times it was Hard Work, Hard Work & Hard Work. In mid-time it changed to Hard Work & Smart Work are keys to success. And now it is Plan, Do & Review.

Whatever action you will take, it will be based on your planning and whatever planning we do, it will be based on our review. So reviews are and will be an integral part of success formula.

Reviews are an introspective meeting for your success. Review is another form of coaching and mentoring.

REVIEWS HELP YOU TO KEEP IN CHECK

Are we in the right direction?
Are we at the right speed?
What needs to be continued?
What needs to be removed?

What needs to be improved?

Every MNC does a monthly review, quarterly review, half yearly review and annual review. If a MNC follows these steps religiously then why can't you and me follow these?

Review can be with immediate senior or super senior also. He has already travelled the road, which you are travelling. He knows the potholes, curves, the speed breakers and falls on the road. Your boss will never give you wrong advice. His success depends upon your success. If you succeeded then he succeeded. If you fail, he becomes weak. After your parents, one of the persons who will be equally or more happy for your success than you will be your coach/your mentor/your boss.

Even the best of performers in any field will be having his coach/mentor (who will do his review) because there are certain things only your boss can see, and you cannot see.

Let me share an example of the most proactive review ever done. This is the story of a child who went to a store and rang up on phone a lady. (Store owner was listening.) Child said, "I will mow your lawn."

Voice from other side, "Already have a person who is doing it." Child said, "I will additionally wash the car also once in a month." Voice from other side: "No."

Child said, "I will do it at 10 $ less per month."

"No." the reply came, and lady on the other side put the phone down. Shopkeeper felt pity on the child and said, "I will like to offer you the job."

"No, I do not need it. I already have the job. I am the same boy who works at her home. I was just checking if I am replaceable and if she is happy with my services."

Perhaps this is one of the best reviews that happened anywhere.

Sheryl Sandberg (COO, Facebook) recently visited Airbnb to share lessons learned from her years at Facebook and Google.

The question was posed to Sandberg: "What's the number one thing you look for in someone who can scale with a company?" Sandberg's reply.

"Someone who takes feedback well. Because people who can take feedback well are people who can learn and grow quickly."

So do a monthly review with your boss, and take feedback positively. Act on it, and show positive improvement. And that is how you will become the SUPER EMPLOYEE of your organisation.

> "We cannot just sit back and wait for feedback to be offered. Particularly when we are in leadership role. If we want feedback to take root in the culture, we need to explicitly ask for it."
>
> – Ed Batista

Actionable: Be proactive. Go to your boss every month-end and get your performance reviewed.

CHAPTER 45
NEVER END YOUR DAY UNLESS…

"A stitch in time saves nine."

It's good to have monthly, quarterly, half-yearly and annual reviews. What about having a daily review at the end of the day by yourself only? Looking at what all you had planned today? What were your most important goals? Why did you achieve them? Why did you miss them? What were your biggest learnings of the day?

And accordingly you will plan your next day, looking at your goals and learnings. And then action and then again review at the end of the day. And the cycle goes on.

By doing this, you are going one step ahead of many multinational companies which do not do daily reviews. This is just a 10-minute investment in your self-growth.

This way you will be building yourself every day as a coach, as a mentor and as a future leader of the organisation.

This is what the coaches do when they are hired by world class athletes This is what the bosses/leaders do when they are hired by companies.

This is what the consultants do when they are hired by MNCs.

This is one of the most powerful habits you can develop, which will be instrumental in taking your career to great heights.

How you spend your day is a reflection of how you will spend your life.

- **If you achieve daily goals, you will achieve weekly goals.**
- **If you achieve weekly goals, you will achieve monthly goals.**
- **If you achieve monthly goals, you will achieve annual goals.**
- **If you achieve annual goals then you will achieve life time goals.**

But all this will happen when you will review yourself daily.

If you don't achieve daily goals, then this is a warning sign. Wake up calls. Review why you could not achieve daily goals. What distracted you? What have you learned? What precaution will you take?

So your review will keep you alert, keep you awake and will keep you in control. So make it a committed habit and non-negotiable habit to review yourself at day-end for 10–15 minutes, and this consistent habit will be one of the strongest reasons to become the fastest SUPER EMPLOYEE of your organisation.

> **"A review a day will make you a champion on the way."**

Actionable: Let a review at the end of the day be one of your 5 most important goals of the day.

CHAPTER 46
WORK HARD, START EARLY, STAY LATER

"Success is never owned, it's rented. And the rent is due every day."

During my graduation, I used to buy a magazine called *Competition Success Review*, which used to share IAS toppers' interviews every month. IAS means Indian Administrative Services. Officers which run the whole administration of the country. Approximately 15 questions were asked in each issue to IAS toppers. I used to buy this magazine only for the last question (question no. 15) which used to be, "What is the secret to your success?," with a hope that this time answer must be a different one. (Giggles) But to my disappointment, it always used to be hard work, sincerity and dedication.

Let me share the best secret I have known from the world leader in body building and famous Hollywood star Arnold Schwarzenegger. I was reading Arnold Schwarzenegger's book *Total Recall* in which he shared that people often asked him what the secret to his amazingly muscular body was. Now comes the secret. Arnold used to tell them, "My secret is 6 hours of gym every day for 5 days a week." Well does that sound like something new? Again hard work. There is no secret, man.

My boss Prateek Mittal's favourite advice to the sales team is, "Success is never owned, it's rented. And the rent is due every day."

One of the most powerful lesson I have learned from my seniors is, "The man who does more than he is paid for, will soon be paid for More than he does." So when you are in the early stages of life, work hard and hard and hard. Be thankful if you are given a harder job than you like; razor cannot be sharpened on a piece of velvet.

Elon Musk (CEO, Tesla) very beautifully said, "Work like Hell. I mean you just have to put 80–100 hours weeks every week. This improves odds of success. If other people are putting in 40 hours workweeks and you are putting in 100 hours workweeks, then even if you are doing the same thing, you know that you will achieve in four months what it takes them to achieve in a year." Try to get 3 years' experience in 1 year. Try to walk 1 mile extra when everyone has stopped. Try to work 1 hour extra when everyone has left office. Work works. Start early, Stay later, Work hard, Party hard.

And that is how you will become the SUPER EMPLOYEE of your organisation. There is no other secret, my dear.

My whole life I had been in search of secret for success, secret for prosperity and secret for luck. And in the end, I could find only one. I am sure you would like to know about it. Turn to the next page.

Harder you work, luckier you become!

CHAPTER 47
MAGIC PILL BEFORE YOU SLEEP

"You become what you think about most of the time."

– Brian Tracy

Sorry. Sorry to share, there are no magic pills in this world. Let's get real. This is again a discipline to be exercised every day exactly before you sleep. And the name of this discipline is affirmations. Before moving ahead, I will request you to read and understand chapter 11 of Section A (Most powerful law of success). Only after that you will make the best out of this chapter.

SO WHAT ARE AFFIRMATIONS?
As per an article in blog successconciousness.com. by Remez Sasson, affirmations are sentences aimed to affect the conscious and the subconscious mind. The words composing the affirmation, automatically and involuntarily, bring up related mental images into the mind, which could inspire, energise and motivate.

HOW DO AFFIRMATIONS HELP?
Helps in empowering the sub conscious mind. Influences the behaviour, habits, actions.

Helps to increase confidence.

Helps to replace negative with positive.

Do's and Don'ts while making affirmations:
1. Choose words carefully which you want to happen in your life.
2. Eliminate words carefully which you don't want to happen in your life.
3. Try to repeat them at a fixed particular time.

Always use present tense. Because your brain only responds to present tense statements.

Use positive words. Don't use negative words like can't, don't, won't.

Use "I am" concept as discussed in chapter 11 in Section A. Don't use words which exhibit uncertainty like might, perhaps, etc.

Some examples of positive affirmations:
I am the most disciplined employee in my organisation.

I am proactive. I work hard, come early and stay late.

I work with owner's mentality.

I always see opportunity in problem.

And that is why I am the highest paid, fastest growing and most honoured employee in my organisation.

This is just an example. However, you have to customise your affirmation carefully keeping in mind the above Do's and Don'ts.

BEST TIME TO EXERCISE THIS DISCIPLINE

Although you can say affirmations throughout the day, however, the best time to say affirmations is exactly before you go to sleep because whatever you say in affirmations will go to your subconscious mind like an instruction, and your subconscious mind will work all night and will sooner or later manifest your dreams.

I always make it a point to do affirmations with my daughter Vrinda before we sleep to help her grow up as a happy, confident and successful daughter in whatever she wants to do in her life.

So choose your words carefully. Eliminate what you don't want from your vocabulary. Repeat them often. Practise affirmations all day along with other success principles. Always practise your customised affirmations just before you sleep. Do it every day. One day this seed will grow up to become a fruit-bearing tree, and that is how you will become the SUPER EMPLOYEE of your organisation.

> "I AM – two of the most powerful words.
> For what you put after them shapes your reality."

Actionable: Do your affirmations daily, just before you are going to sleep.

CHAPTER 48
SELF-DISCIPLINE AND ACCOUNTABILITY

"World is full of talented unsuccessful people."

Do you know one of the most important and missing ingredients in success recipe? It's not knowledge, it's not skill, it's not desire… It's discipline. Self-discipline. We all are knowledgeable. We know everything that should be done, still we don't do it.

People say, "Neeraj Sir, fill this guy with motivation, just make him a fired-up guy." No. Motivation can only help you to get started. Beyond a point, you will get distracted, and you will feel like postponing it, there you need discipline and nothing else. I had worked in an insulin selling company called Biocon, where I learned how Type 1 Diabetic patients must inject insulin via injectables 2–3 times a day for their whole lives. If someone is Type 1 Diabetic, does he need motivation to insert insulin injection every day? No. Period. You only need discipline to do it. Whether you like it or not.

My favourite definition on discipline is, "Discipline is the ability to do what should be done whether you like it or not."

Journey to success is full of disciplines and sacrifices. You have to make many short-term sacrifices in order to achieve long-term success.

Here I will share one of the best lessons of my life which I learned from my boss Prateek Mittal, who learned it from his father whom we call Bade Sir. Once I asked Prateek Sir, "You are so young, just 29. You have not missed any Sunday in the last 8 years in this company. I never saw you in jeans or T shirt in the last 5 years. I never saw you going for disco parties or anything. Don't you have an urge for this type of lifestyle once a while?"

He shared with me the story which his father (Bade Sir) told him. Bade Sir said, "Chandragupta Maurya (reign: 321–298 BCE) was having a dream of uniting the whole of India and becoming the emperor of United India." To a great extent, he was successful in that. He was on his way to attack a country. Royal family of that country got the news in advance, and they left the palace before the attack. Destiny had a different game plan. Chandragupta Maurya met the same royal family on the way and fell in love with a female servant of the princess of the royal family. Later, Chandragupta Maurya came to know that the female servant was actually the princess who disguised as the female servant because of security reason. Now Chandragupta Maurya was in a dilemma, as he was in love with the daughter of the enemy. It was duty vs. love. Chandragupta Maurya asked his mentor Chanakya, "Is love wrong? Is it inhuman to fall in love?"

Chanakya (his guru) said, "I have not given you this part of training. Ok. There is nothing wrong with falling in love with someone. But yes it is wrong for a person who is having dream of uniting the whole of India (Akahand Bharat) and dreaming of becoming the emperor of the country. In this case, this is distraction from your focus of life's biggest goal for country and mankind. So for big dreams, the sacrifices also have to be big."

So if you want to be the no. 1 team, no. 1 manager or SUPER EMPLOYEE of your organisation then you should be ready to discipline your life and make many sacrifices. If you want to be an average employee then do everything and anything. If you don't sacrifice for what you want, what you want becomes the sacrifice.

There is no alternative to discipline. It will always remain there. Only question is who will exercise it. You have first choice to discipline yourself or else your boss will discipline you.

So be disciplined in thinking, habits, action and planning. Love the word discipline. Be proud to see yourself disciplined. Discipline to make sacrifices, discipline for early start, discipline to persist more, discipline to say NO, discipline to stay focused, and that is how you will become the SUPER EMPLOYEE of your organisation.

> "Discipline is the bridge between dreams and accomplishment."

CHAPTER 49
NEVER GIVE UP

"Never give up. Today is hard, tomorrow will be worse,
but the day after tomorrow will be sunshine."

– Jack Ma

Surprisingly, one of the biggest reasons for failure to achieve your goal is the act of giving up when you are quite near your goal. If you will stay in the game for a little more time, if you will bear that pain for a little more time, if you will believe in yourself for a little more time and if you will not give up, you are bound to succeed. You will live your dream.

Let me share an amazing story of Marvan Attapattu, Sri Lankan Cricketer, which is a perfect testimony to this. It's a story that Harsha Bhogle, India's most loved cricket commentator, loves to tell over and over again.

Making his debut in test cricket for Sri Lanka, Marvan scored a duck in his first innings. And again, in his second innings.

They dropped him. So he went back to the nets for more practice. More first-class cricket. More runs. Waiting for that elusive call. And after twenty-one months, he got a second chance.

This time, he tried harder. His scores: 0 in the first innings, 1 in the second dropped again, he went back to the grind and scored tonnes of runs in first-class cricket. Runs that seemed inadequate to erase the painful memories of the Test failures.

Well, seventeen months later, opportunity knocked yet again. Marvan got to bat in both innings of the Test. His scores: 0 and 0. Phew! Back to the grind. Would the selectors ever give him another chance? They said he lacked big-match temperament. His technique wasn't good enough at the highest level. Undaunted, Marvan kept trying.

Three years later, he got another chance. This time, he made runs. He came good. And in an illustrious career thereafter, Marvan went on to score over 5000 runs for Sri Lanka. That included sixteen centuries and six double hundreds. And he went on to captain his country. All this despite taking over six years to score his second run in test cricket.

Wow! What a guy! How many of us can handle failure as well as he did? Six years of trying and failing. He must have been tempted to pursue another career. Change his sport perhaps. Play county cricket. Or, oh well, just give up. But he didn't. And that made the difference.

The next time you are staring at a possible failure or rejection, think of Marvan. And remember this: If you don't give up, if you believe in yourself, if you stay the course, the run will eventually come. What's more, you could even become captain someday. One more thing, Marvan is a qualified Sri Lankan chartered accountant.

NEVER GIVE UP!
NEVER, NEVER GIVE UP!! PROVE THEM WRONG!

There will be times when you will feel like losing faith, losing hope and giving up. Everyone who is working on his goal seriously goes through the same phase. I suggest that whenever you feel like giving up, go back to Chapter 1: What is your Why? Remember the Why behind that dream, and you will get a magical power to continue your journey.

The only ones who are remembered by history are the ones who don't give up. Let me share with you some real life heroes, who despite all odds didn't give up and made their dream a reality, and that's why they are remembered as heroes & game changers.

REAL LIFE SUCCESS STORY NO. 1

During birth, a wrong gynaecological procedure caused him to have one sided paralysis. Faced lot of mockery in school days. Growing up he dreamt of having a career in movies. Soon a time came when he went broke. Under heavy debt. Sold his wife's jewellery. Wife was pregnant. Went homeless. Slept at New York bus station for 3 days. Had to sell his favourite dog for 25 $ for his better care. After getting inspired from a boxing match he wrote a script of a movie. Another challenge was that he wanted to act in that film as a main lead. More than 1000 production houses refused him. Quite logical to give up at this time.

Finally one studio offered him 2,50,000 for just the script and not him. He refused. Soon they offered him 3,50,000 for just the script and not him. He refused.

Pressure was great on him to accept the offer, and it would be mad to refuse it. He still refused. He didn't give up. They gave him 35000 $ for the script and have him as the lead star.

The rest as they say is history. 1 million $ was spent on making the movie, and earnings from this movie were around 200 million $. It won the Oscar for Best Picture, Best Direction and Best Film Editing. The movie was Rocky, and you know the person as Sylvester Stallone. Because he did not give up. And by the way, you know what he did with the first $35,000?

He stood outside the liquor store, where he sold his dog for 3 days, identified the man who had bought it and finally got him back for $15,000. The whole world knows him by the name Sylvester Stallone because he didn't give up.

REAL LIFE SUCCESS STORY NO. 2

He was rejected from 30 jobs including KFC. When KFC entered China, KFC took interview of 24 people, 23 were selected, only he was rejected. Failed 2 times in school in class 4. Failed 3 times in class 8. Failed 5 times in graduation entrance exams. Rejected from Harvard 10 times. Quite logical to give up. But he didn't. He stayed in the game, and few years later he became one of the most powerful businessman of China with net worth of more than 23.7 billion $. You know him as Jack Ma founder of Ali Baba Group because he didn't give up.

REAL LIFE SUCCESS STORY NO. 3

She was born to a housemaid and coal worker. Raped at 9 & 13. Pregnant at 14. Quite logical to give up. But she didn't. She stayed in the game and became a millionaire by 32. Titled "QUEEN OF ALL MEDIA." Net worth 3.2 billion $. One of the most influential women of USA. Whole world knows her by the name of Oprah Winfrey because she didn't give up.

REAL LIFE SUCCESS STORY NO. 4

Jobless lady. Single mother. Fought depression. Took couple of years to complete her 1st book. Got rejected by 12 publishers. Quite logical to give up.

But she didn't. She stayed in the game and eventually become the richest author and first author to become a billionaire from her Harry Potter series. Whole world knows her as J K Rowling because she didn't give up.

REAL LIFE SUCCESS STORY NO. 5

This brand sold only 25 bottles in the first year. Quite logical to give up.

But they didn't give up, and today they are world leaders. We know that brand as Coca Cola because they didn't give up.

REAL LIFE SUCCESS STORY NO. 6

His father died when he was 5. His mother married another man. He left school. He left home. By the age of 17 he was fired from 4 jobs. Married at 18. Worked as bus conductor for 4 years. Then joined army and was fired from army. Tried to enter law school but was rejected. Joined Life Insurance co. but was unsuccessful. Wife left him at 20. Worked as cook in hotel. Retired at age of 65. On the 1st day of retirement he received a cheque from the Government for $105. He felt that the Government was saying that he couldn't provide for himself. He decided to commit suicide, it wasn't worth living anymore; he had failed so much. Quite logical to give up.

However, he didn't. He realised there was much more that he hadn't done. There was one thing he could do better than anyone he knew. And that was how to cook delicious fried chicken.

With little in terms of means at his disposal, he travelled door to door to houses and restaurants all over his local area. He wanted to partner with someone to help promote his chicken recipe.

He started travelling by car to different restaurants and cooked his fried chicken on the spot for restaurant owners. If the owner liked the chicken, they would enter into a handshake agreement to sell his chicken recipe. It is said that 1009 people rejected him.

Quite logical to give up. But he didn't give up and then 1010th person gave him a chance. Then others, then more and more and more, and today his company is operating in more than 120 countries with more than 18000 outlets worldwide. Remember at age 65 he was ready to commit suicide, but at age 88, he was a billionaire.

His company's name is Kentucky Fried chicken (KFC), and we all know him by the name Col. Sanders because he didn't give up.

If you look carefully at the lives of all super successful people then you will find that all super successful people were actually super failures who didn't give up.

Journey to SUPER EMPLOYEE might be filled with sacrifices, commitments, blood, tears and sweat. But if you hang in there, if you remember your Why, if you Never give up, then we will see you at the TOP, and YOU WILL EVENTUALLY BECOME THE SUPER EMPLOYEE OF YOUR ORGANISATION.

> "Remember why you started, hang in there & don't give up, and you will do it. GOD BLESS."
>
> – Neeraj Bali

In my Next Book, I will be sharing Spiritual Laws to Become the SUPER EMPLOYEE.
Stay Connected with me on
Facebook, Twitter & Instagram on following IDs.

---

neeraj.bali.39 | NeerajBali15 | neerajbali13

www.ingramcontent.com/pod-product-compliance
Lightning Source LLC
Chambersburg PA
CBHW030925180526
45163CB00002B/461